THE LUBICON LAKE NATION:
INDIGENOUS KNOWLEDGE AND POWER

Many argue that the Lubicon, a small Cree nation in northern Alberta, have been denied their unalienable right to self-determination by the Canadian government. In a country such as Canada, some see the plight of the Lubicon people as an enduring reminder that certain democratic principles and basic freedoms are still kept from minorities, Indigenous groups in particular.

The Lubicon Lake Nation strives, through a critique of historically constructed colonial images, to analyse the Canadian government's actions vis-à-vis the rights of the Lubicon people. In this ambitious work Dawn Martin-Hill illustrates the power of Indigenous knowledge by contrasting the words, ideas, and self-conceptualizations of the Lubicon with official versions of Lubicon history as documented by the state. In doing so, she offers a genuine sense of the gravity of their lived experiences as a cultural minority. By giving voice to the Lubicon, this study seeks to develop an exclusively Indigenist framework in which the circumstances facing the people can be described more accurately than they can using popular conceptions of Native rights as put forth by the government.

The Lubicon Lake Nation is the story of one culture and its pursuit of Indigenous rights in Canada as told from the perspective of those who know it best, the Lubicon themselves.

DAWN MARTIN-HILL is a cultural anthropologist and academic director of the Indigenous Studies Program at McMaster University.

D1069414

DAWN MARTIN-HILL

The Lubicon Lake Nation

Indigenous Knowledge and Power

UNIVERSITY OF TORONTO PRESS
Toronto Buffalo London

© University of Toronto Press Incorporated 2008
www.utppublishing.com
Toronto Buffalo London
Printed in Canada

ISBN 978-0-8020-0843-5 (cloth)
ISBN 978-0-8020-7828-5 (paper)

Printed on acid-free paper

Library and Archives Canada Cataloguing in Publication

.Martin-Hill, Dawn, 1962–

The Lubicon Lake Nation : indigenous knowledge and power / Dawn
Martin-Hill.

ISBN 978-0-8020-0843-5 (bound)
ISBN 978-0-8020-7828-5 (pbk.)

1. Lubicon Lake Indian Nation – History.   2. Lubicon Lake Indian
Nation – Historiography.   3. Cree Indians – Alberta – Lubicon Lake
Region – History.   4. Cree Indians – Alberta – Lubicon Lake
Region – Historiography.   5. Cree philosophy.   6. Cree Indians –
Government relations.   7. Indians of North America – Canada –
Government relations.   I. Title.

E99.C88M374 2007   971.23'100497323   C2007-903198-6

This book has been published with the help of a grant from the Canadian
Federation for the Humanities and Social Sciences, through the Aid to
Scholarly Publications Programme, using funds provided by the Social
Sciences and Humanities Research Council of Canada.

University of Toronto Press acknowledges the financial assistance to its
publishing program of the Canada Council for the Arts and the Ontario
Arts Council.

University of Toronto Press acknowledges the financial support for its
publishing activities of the Government of Canada through the Book
Publishing Industry Development Program (BPIDP).

Contents

Foreword

The first time I heard of the Lubicon was in 1987, when I read about them in the *Saturday Evening Post*. I related to everything Chief Ominayak had to say about their land. I saw him as standing up for his people's rights to the land and I remember feeling for them. Their contact with white people had been a very short time in comparison to the length of time that our people have had contact. I remember thinking it gave me more heart to see a leader standing up for his people and I thought some day in time I would like to meet him. At that time I was only twenty-seven, but I had been active in my seat on the Confederacy Council for ten years, regularly attending meetings. I had actually been stood up by my mother at four years old. Having been put in that position at such a young age my mother made sure I attended all the Nation meetings and I had become very close to the old people. The title I held was one of the first titles in the founding of the Six Nations Confederacy, Tekarihoken, who was one of the first leaders to accept the Great Peace, more than two thousand years ago. I was raised with the old leaders who were very passionate for their people and their fight for justice, but at the same time they were very soft-spoken people. That's just the way I was brought up; it was my job to fulfil that role. Bernard Ominayak reminded me of all those things – what I would like to see Native leadership do, to stand up for our morals, values, and heritage. I first had the opportunity to meet Bernard in person in 1989, when he was brought to Six Nations, Grand River Territory, to meet with the Confederacy Chiefs and Clanmothers. I was very pleased to meet him. He talked too quietly. When I asked him why, he responded, 'People will have to listen closely.' He was presenting his treaty alliance, and at that time the Chiefs were not ready to sign a document so they agreed to burn tobacco as a sacred agreement between us and them, to help each other. I accepted him as a brother, a brother nation, and told him that if he ever needed anything he should come through us, the Mohawk Nation. We discussed our principles and the principles of the Two Row Wampum and he agreed with our approach to coexistence with our white brothers. And so that was the beginning of an alliance between the Lubicon and the Confederacy. Through this alliance Bernard was embraced as a brother, and given a name by the Mohawks. It was 1990 when I first visited Little Buffalo. Over the course of the next four years I visited a number of times. That first time, I remember we went up to Fish Lake to participate in their ceremonies and a wild horse walked right through the ceremonial grounds. This was the beginning of many spiritual exchanges. So I went into the lodge with my towel and waited. I looked out and saw all these women. One of the older men asked, 'Is this how you always go in the lodge,' I said 'Yes.' He asked if I wanted to conduct the ceremony. I said 'No.' There were many comical and heartwarming moments. We endeared ourselves with the differences in our cultures, which often resulted in great laughter. An Elder said to me, 'I had a vision for your people.' I asked, 'What was it?' He said, 'Give me ten horses first.' I never gave the horses and I never got the vision. Our playful banter was that of an older and younger brother; in this way we were like brothers. The spirituality and the laughter became the essence that filled our hearts. Our role was really significant to them because of our long stand for sovereignty and autonomy. Our job was to uplift each other, our minds and our spirits. This relationship extends back to the Peacemaker and the founding of the League of Peace. Today, 2006, the issues of the Lubicon and the land still exist, as well as the issues of the Haudenosaunee. Today, I find myself still at the front lines of our struggles, this time in Caledonia. For more than two hundred years the land rights of Indigenous peoples have not been dealt with fairly. The process of colonization continues, we bring forward our concerns on encroachment and we are told by the colonial governments that there is nothing that can be done to stop it. Today we have a crisis across our lands. Our people are taking a stand and insisting that it is time to make change; this is happening all across the western hemisphere. I can only hope that Western society has come to a level of enlightenment where they can offer to come to terms with the injustices done to the Indigenous peoples of this land and what has been done to the land itself, the misuse and destruction of the source of all life. This book honours the legacy of Indigenous peoples, the Lubicon and their relationship to the Haudenosaunee Confederacy and our homelands. It is my hope you walk away from this work with a deeper sense of our people, our struggle, and our rights. That you act to restore honour and peace in these lands we all call home. Donanto.

Chief Tekarihoken
Mohawk Nation

Preface

This book will develop an Indigenist framework and demonstrate its application to an Indigenous people – namely, the Lubicon Lake Cree Nation. Its overriding objective is to demonstrate the power of Indigenous Knowledge as it is exemplified by the Lubicon people. From the perspective of the Lubicon Cree, it is constructed in a way that demands obligation, stewardship, and justice. The Lubicon, a small nation in northern Alberta, Canada, possess the inherent right to live as they choose, unmolested and in peace. Yet the most basic human rights in a democracy such as Canada have been denied to them by the state. This book will make it clear how the Canadian government has failed to apply its own laws, democratic principles, and justice system, and what the consequences have been, and continue to be, for a quiet and peaceful Cree people.

I especially want to humanize the Lubicon people – men, women, children, and Elders. I want to reveal who they are and what their experiences have been fighting the state-sponsored development projects of multinational corporations. Past accounts of Indigenous peoples' struggles for land have often focused on Eurocentric representations that emphasize economics and the law. Such an approach too often naturalizes Indigenous human suffering at the hands of industries that are claiming to offer development and progress. As we enter an era of globalization, the offspring of imperialism, governments are promoting unjust practices, the contention being that development is in the country's best interests. But who really benefits?

I intend to examine how the West has constructed its images of Aboriginal people – images that have served to justify, objectify, and naturalize genocidal practices and policies. Many decades ago, scientific authorities in the West systematically 'proved' that Aboriginal people were 'inferior' in evolutionary terms – a conclusion founded on twisted European values. Through policies of oppression – such as relocation, the seizure of land and resources, and forced residential schooling – the West benefited greatly from the sufferings it inflicted on Indigenous populations. The West's view was that Indigenous peoples were incapable of intellectual thought, nor could they make their own social, political, and economic arrangements. This view is what justified laws that essentially stripped Indigenous populations of their human rights and of their right to be Indigenous. Today, those Indigenous scholars who are constructing Indigenous Knowledge (instead of wasting precious time deconstructing Western paradigms) have arrived at a historical moment: they are repositioning Indigenous people as the experts within Indigenous Knowledge frameworks. Placing the knowledge, the stories, and the truth of the Lubicon Cree in a humanized context has provided me with an Indigenous 'point of reference' for this research.

In the first chapter, I articulate and critique the problems that anthropological theories and frameworks continue to pose for accurate representations of the 'other.' This is a necessary exercise for those who have no knowledge of how Eurocentric assumptions have come to pervade North American views of Indigenous people. After this, I take on a more critical task: to explain the epistemological foundations of an Indigenous paradigm. This is the spirit, the very heart, of the work. Indigenous theory and methodology will emerge from my discussion of Haudenosaunee principles and will then be embellished by the Lubicon in their own (Cree) representations of their history and contemporary reality, representations that move far beyond legal economic rhetoric. The chapters that follow include the *official* versions of Lubicon history as documented by the state and its bureaucracies. Juxtaposed with the official versions is the Indigenist account of Lubicon history. The voices include my own and those of Lubicon men, women, Elders, and children, as well as commentaries from Elders from Haudenosaunee territory. The dialogue and relationships created by the Indigenous framework employed here will demonstrate clearly the dynamics of Indigenous Knowledge and power.

The Lubicon voices will be making the richest contribution to this book. Through their own words and ideas, and through their conceptualizations of their own social, political, and spiritual world, readers will come to appreciate the power of their lived experiences. The costs of fighting off multinational developments and struggling for survival have been very high. They are the heroes of this book.

I hope to leave readers with a strong sense of responsibility and accountability for achieving social justice for the Lubicon. Readers, students, and intellectuals who do nothing as global citizens will be inflicting the gravest injustice, ethnocide.

Aboriginal scholars recognize that scholarship can be used to restore justice and to reclaim a reality that has for too long been hidden behind ethnocentric assumptions about the 'Indian problem.' This book is a call to consciousness and to action. It is also a bid to prove that scholarship is not a hollow exercise, but one that can challenge historically constructed colonial images. The Lubicon children deserve no less.

On a personal note, what has happened since my research ended in Little Buffalo in 1993 is too extraordinary to recount here. The impact the Lubicon had on my intellectual, emotional, and spiritual psyche has been simple yet profound. I haven't the words to express how much the Lubicon have reshaped my consciousness; what I can say is that they left a deep impression that led me on a quest to find solutions to the problems encountered by most Indigenous peoples. Leaving Little Buffalo in 1993 was difficult and yet very necessary. Knowing that it is time to leave and actually doing it are two very different things. On leaving, I set out to assist the Lubicon from an outsider position – mainly because being inside had begun to overwhelm my own sense of power, thus rendering me useless to their situation as well as to my own. In the past decade I have stayed in touch with the Lubicon but I have also broadened my work with grassroots movements. This in turn has influenced the intellectual groundwork for this book. I have regained my own sense of power and am striving to utilize all that I have learned to form a meaningful framework for the Lubicon field research.

As a professor and academic director of Indigenous Studies, I have learned firsthand how difficult it is for us to survive and thrive in Western institutions that show little respect for, or are inhospitable to, indigenous people and their knowledge. Over and over again, we are faced with the enormous task of asking permission to exist, and meanwhile we must search for tools that will validate us as worthy of such privilege. If the Lubicon have shown me anything, it is how to tap our collective strength, determination, and will to survive in spite of all odds. The Lubicon will no doubt provide many of our people with inspiration and teachings for many years to come. I say niawenko:wa to all those Lubicon Cree in northern Alberta.

This is for you Mom; you are loved and missed so much.

Acknowledgments

To our teachers, the Elders: First and foremost, niá:wen to all the Elders who have travelled to the spirit world, including my own grandmother and mother. Niá:wen to my own mentor, Henry Joe, and the many good people who have surrounded this work: Summer Joe, Edward Laboucon, Reg Henry, Thomas Banyacya, Leon Shenendoah, Jake Thomas, Cassie Jacobs, Oliver Jacobs, and Albert Laboucon. And niá:wen to those still with us, Bertha Skye, Hubert Skye, Arnold General, Norma General, Sara Smith, John C. and Birgil Kills Straight, Fraser and Frank Andrew, Paul George, Ernest Sundown, and Sylvia Maracle.

To the Lubicon, to Jennifer Ominayak, Maggie Auger, Rosanna Gladue, Louise Ominayak, and the Lubicon Women's Circle, to Chief Bernard Ominayak and Council, to the Elders Council, and to all the children, many nyá:wen. I hope this book has done all your hard work, knowledge, and wisdom some justice. Niá:wen also to the Indigenous Elders and Youth Council, Amazon Conservation Team, National Aboriginal Health Organization, Indigenous Health Research Development Program, Ontario Indian Federation of Friendship Centres, Hamilton Regional Indian Centre, Aboriginal Healing Foundation, and Six Nations Polytechnic and Ansihnawbe Health Centre. And thanks must go to the current work of the International Indigenous Elders Summit, which brought Lubicon Elders and youth to the Indigenous community, and to the Six Nations Trust Fund, Dreamcatchers, and Heritage Canada. A special thanks to the Clanmothers of Six Nations: Kathy Smoke, Louise McDonald, Bernice Johnson, Mina Key, Mary Sandy, Eileen Jacobs, Frances Froman, Lucille Jameson.

Friends, family, and coworkers: Six Nations family and friends are far too numerous to list here. To my children, Amber, Ashley, Makasa, and

Cody, and granddaughter Aleena, thank you for sharing your mom. Each of you had to sacrifice in many ways so that this work could be finished. You are all my reason for being, and without you I should cease to be.

Niá:wen to the Hills, especially the late Allen and Bernice, for all your support. And to the Looking Horses, the late Stanley and Cecelia, whose wisdom humbled me. And to Arvol and the Looking Horse family for continued support. And to Mikey Peters and the Pratt family for your spiritual support. And to the many strong women ... you're missed. And to Bertha Skye for holding me together when my mom passed away. And to Faithkeeper Elva Jamieson, niá:wen for your strength which carried us. And to Wendy McNaughton, Pat Hess, Janet Hill, Roxanne Skye, Theresa and Honey McCarthy, Linda Staats, Katsi Cook, and Clanmother Louise McDonald, niá:wen. To coworkers Danielle Soucy, Cassandra Pohl, and Valerie O'Brien, niá:wen for helping me finish this among other things. And to James Lamouche and Lana Whiskey Jack for all the moral support and beautiful artwork. And to Marion Murdock and your son 'Stuff' for all of your help. And to my sister Debi Jamieson, the children's shining light. And to my special brother, Danny, who knows more than most, many niá:wen. Also, to the 'Anishnawbe allies' – Alexandra Darnay you're awesome, and to the King family and Sundancers, niá:wen for your unconditional support. Niá:wen to all the students who have taught me and who have inspired me all these years to keep going. A special nya:wen to Spirit of the Youth for all your hard work and dedication. Niá:wen to the Elders Summit Committee, and to the Haudenosaunee Clanmothers and Women for nurturing community healing and unity.

The Academic Community: Niá:wen to a great mentor, Harvey Feit, and to the McMaster Presidents Committee on Indigenous Issues, and to the Social Sciences and Humanities Research Council, for their research support. And niá:wen to the Fulbright Foundation, Dr Konrad, and the Canada Council for the Arts for their support of Indigenous Knowledge research.

University of Toronto Press editor Virgil Duff, why you signed me in 1992 I'll never know. You waited more than fourteen years patiently, just like a grandfather – many, many niá:wen for your support.

Confederacy Chief Arnold General and Allan McNaughton visiting Little Buffalo, 1992.

THE LUBICON LAKE NATION:
INDIGENOUS KNOWLEDGE AND POWER

Introduction: Indigenous Knowledge –
The Haudenosaunee and Lubicon

Positioning the Author(s)

So many of our older people have influenced this work, the research, the analysis; it is a collective effort and therefore ownership of the work cannot be claimed by one person. Elders from Lubicon, Six Nations, and the western prairies have touched the thinking, the patterns, and the work in ways both big and small.

With the passing of my mother, many of them contacted me. 'It is time,' they said. Then the word came from the Chief of the Lubicon as well. It had been six years since I last worked on rewriting my doctoral dissertation. Perhaps the subtle nudge from the community had something to do with their sense that I was mature enough to represent them. People seemed to want the book; all of a sudden they felt it was time.

If there is a 'rite of passage' for the Indigenous intellectual, it has certainly been my path for the past several years. Since 1993, I have lost my grandmother, mother, grandfathers, my marriage, and my home, as well as cherished Elders. I have also had two beautiful babies and now have four mouths to feed. Life had been getting in the way of this book, and I was grieving for all the losses. However, it was time.

Looking back, I find that I have gained an appreciation for all of the people involved in this work that was absent several years ago. Perhaps it was my own disposition; it had to do with humbling myself enough to appreciate the full gravity of shared experiences and the Elders' words. It can be best explained in the way that the PhD initially seemed to mean little to me or my community. However, through this work I have earned a certain approval from those I hold in high esteem. They watched to see whether I would exploit my heritage and my people, or appropriate or pervert their knowledge. I hope I have not. I remained a student long after the PhD and formal research were 'officially' completed – the real work and learning had just begun. From 1993 until the present, a process of coming to terms with my own pain, character faults, weaknesses, and limitations became clear. However, I have also reflected on the overall strengths of Mohawk women. Beginning to heal from the legacies of colonialism involved a mental, physical, spiritual, and emotional transformation that has altered my consciousness. That life-changing journey began in Little Buffalo, Alberta, with the Lubicon.

Acknowledging the very real pain associated with Indigenous peoples' realities is crucial to thinking clearly about how we came to be in the position we are in today. As an Indigenous woman and researcher, it is vital for me to analyse 'our position' in this country and in our families, communities, and institutions. The impact of missionaries, residential schools, the Indian Act, and colonialism in general on generations of women has been severe; this is the position from which I speak. The effects of colonialism on the social, political, economic, and spiritual well-being of Indigenous women have been profound. The authority and the esteemed positions that Indigenous women once held in their societies have been severely eroded. A glimpse of our profile as a gender and race in this country will illustrate the context in which I am positioned, whether in Little Buffalo or Six Nations. Let me introduce the world in which I tried to do research.

Three-quarters of Aboriginal women have been the victim of family violence: over 55 per cent reported physical abuse and 31.8 per cent reported sexual abuse (Grace 2002, 368). Native women have on average 3.7 children, unlike their non-Native counterparts, who have 2.1 children (Frideres and Gadacz 2005, 70). Aboriginal women are raising large families, and Aboriginal women aged between fifteen and twenty-four are three times more likely to be single mothers than Canadian women of the same age (Norris et al. 2003, 19). The income of status families averages $21,800, which is 'about half that of the average Canadian family of $38,000' (Frideres and Gadacz 2005, 100). Less than 5 per cent of Aboriginal people have a university degree, compared to 16 per cent of non-Aboriginal people (ibid., 118). Living conditions reflect these statistics. Three-quarters of all existing housing (on reserve) fails to meet basic standards of living. While only 2 per cent of Canadians live in overcrowded conditions, more than one-third of Native people live in overcrowded conditions (ibid., 85–6). Aboriginal women are also disproportionately represented in incarceration admissions in comparison to non-Aboriginal women in all provinces. Women account for 5 per cent of all inmates in Canadian correctional facilities. One-quarter of those imprisoned women are Aboriginal, yet less than 3 per cent of Canadians are Aboriginals (ibid., 138–9). The life expectancy of Aboriginal people is more than six years less than the Canadian average (ibid., 70). A recent publication by Amnesty International, reveals that according to 1996 statistics, 'Indigenous women between the ages of 25 and 44 with status under the Federal Indian Act, are five times more likely than other women of the same age to die as the result of violence' (Amnesty International 2004, 23). According to AI's report, *Stolen Sisters: Discrimination and Violence against Indigenous Women in Canada*:

> NWAC believes that the incidents that have come to light are only part of the picture. The organization has estimated that over the past twenty years more than five hundred Indigenous women may have been murdered or gone missing in circumstances suggesting violence ... The resulting vulnerability of Indigenous women has been exploited by Indigenous and non-Indigenous men to carry out acts of extreme brutality against Indigenous women [and] these acts of violence may be motivated by racism, or may be carried out in the expectation that societal indifference to the welfare and safety of Indigenous women will allow the perpetrators to escape justice. (ibid., 5–6)

However grim the social profile of Aboriginal women in this country, we are not victims. We are not wounded beings. Indigenous women are seeking ways to repair and rebuild their families and their traditional positions (Anderson 2000; Gunn Allen 1986). Within the framework of what it means to be an Aboriginal woman in this country – a framework that includes racism and sexism – I have come to appreciate the fact that without my community, I could never have done this work.

So what does this have to do with the Lubicon women? Everything. To illustrate, the philosophy of the Peacemaker promoted strength through unity; the Peacemaker himself chose women to uphold the Great Law by creating the position of Clanmothers (Wright 1992, 223–38; Lyons and Mohawk 1992, 1–13). The Haudenosaunee operated their society on intellectually advanced principles. Only recently, however, have scholars in the West examined the First Americans as interdependent societies with autonomous political, social, and economic structures. Even more recent scholarship has considered the position of women. It is important for this literature to acknowledge both the past contributions of Indigenous women to the Nation and the issues they must confront today – in particular, the racism and sexism that so often distinguish their agenda from that of other 'feminist' projects. First and foremost, Indigenous women are seeking to reintegrate traditional structures with their communities, to heal their families, and to renegotiate those positions of authority that were stripped from them through legal frameworks such as the Indian Act (Green and Bass 1998; Monture-Angus 1999; Anderson 2000).

That Indigenous peoples, consciously or not, have adopted Western patriarchal ideologies is worth acknowledging. The best indicator of how patriarchy has transformed traditional Indigenous systems is Indigenous women's economic status and social standing. Anderson, Gunn Allen, and McGillivray and Comaskey have all assessed both as profoundly troubling. Edward Said (1989) referred to this as 'epistemic violence.' We live there.

It is important that I emphasize the realities facing Aboriginal women before I move on to the Lubicon and Indigenous Knowledge. Most Indigenous scholars do not live in cocoons away from the realities of their communities. With all due respect, I am not nearly as privileged as my colleagues. I am a minority within the majority. I *have* the life experiences that they study, examine, and write about but that they do not *live*. This reality has shaped my research at every conceivable level. Aboriginal people live in the shadow of colonialism; on top of this, Aboriginal women must contend with violence and sexism in their own communities as well as racism and marginalization in academic institutions. Some non-Native academics refuse to respect Indigenous Knowledge or women; at least as many Aboriginal people reject and disregard their communities' own knowledge, especially that of women.

From this overview, one can begin to understand the everyday obstacles faced by Aboriginal women. What does it mean to be a Mohawk anthropologist? I still do not know. Professionally, I have been identified as the first Mohawk anthropologist in Canada. There is no home for us at universities or in academia in general. Being the first of anything is little short of a nightmare. There is no map, no trail, there are no familiar faces. We are forced to be administrators, mentors, activists, committee members, community representatives, and more, but not researchers, intellectuals, or academics. Quitting is always on one's mind. For whatever good has come to me in the academy, I can only thank the Creator and the strength of the Indigenous women in my family and in Little Buffalo. I owe it to their guidance, love, and support.

At Six Nations, the community in which I still live, the women supported my university education and research goals. Because of my tribal kinship system, I was able to continue this work. Six Nations community members came to Little Buffalo with me to support the people. All of them opened their doors to my family when we had no home. They piled into a small room at McMaster to support me during my dissertation defence. As an individual, I am powerless. What power I do have arises from being a Mohawk woman, Onkwehonwe – a 'real human being.' My grandmother, mother, and I – we have all survived the worst that colonialism could inflict on us. This is new for us. That I have earned a PhD, do social science research, have become an anthropologist, teach at a university, and am writing a book – it's all new and somewhat baffling. (And yes, I know there were others before me in the United States, but their frames of reference and mine are very different, for reasons I can't go into here.) It is in my mother's memory and in her honour that I write this book. My gift to my three daughters, my son, and my granddaughter is the gift of an ongoing tribal collective consciousness. I hope that I have instilled in them a sense of social justice. My goal is to show them that colonialism is not what we are but what we must overcome.

Making the Case for Indigenous Knowledge

Indigenous pedagogy acknowledges diverse ways of knowing and respects the pluralism of knowledge. Geographic and cultural diversity is part of Indigenous Knowledge and contributes to our knowledge base. As pointed out in *Protection of the Heritage of Indigenous People* (the Daes Report) written by Dr Erica-Irene Daes for the UN, 'Indigenous knowledge is a complete knowledge system with its own concepts of epistemology, philosophy, and scientific and logical validity ... [which] can only be fully learned or understood by means of the pedagogy traditionally employed by these people themselves' (in Battiste and Youngblood Henderson 2000, 41).

Mohawk scholar Marlene Brant Castellano (2000) suggests that Indigenous Knowledge has multiple sources, including traditional, spiritual, and empirical. Indigenous Knowledge engages a holistic paradigm that acknowledges the emotional, spiritual, physical, and mental well-being of a people. The cultural diversity of Indigenous peoples is addressed through the recognition that Indigenous Knowledge is attached to the language, landscapes, and cultures from which it emerges. Also, Indigenous Knowledge does not subscribe to knowledge hierarchies. Vandana Shiva argues that 'under the colonial influence the biological and intellectual heritage of non-western societies was devalued. The priorities of scientific development ... transformed the plurality of knowledge systems into a hierarchy of knowledge systems. When knowledge plurality mutated into knowledge hierarchy, the horizontal ordering of diverse but equally valid systems was converted into a vertical ordering of unequal systems, and the epistemological foundations of western knowledge were imposed on non-western knowledge systems with the result that the latter were invalidated' (Dei, Hall, and Rosenburg 2000, vii).

Western cultural constructs of 'valid' empirical research have marginalized Indigenous ways of knowing (ibid., Battiste and Youngblood Henderson 2000; L. Smith 1999). In this chapter I develop an Indigenous Knowledge framework in order to address the undermining of Indigenous authority by colonial institutions and their agents, missionaries, and academics.

Indigenous people's relationship to place, to the land, has been well documented by anthropologists. Our very awareness of our place in the universe is informed by the land. But what Indigenous scholars are presenting today moves beyond attachment to the land. These points are elaborated by Battiste and Youngblood Henderson (2000, 41): 'Indigenous peoples regard all products of the human mind and heart as interrelated within Indigenous knowledge. They assert that all knowledge flows from the same source: the relationships between a global flux that needs to be renewed, the people's kinship with the other living creatures that share the land, and the people's kinship with the spirit world. Since the ultimate source of knowledge is the changing ecosystem itself, the art and science of a specific people manifest these relationships and can be considered as manifestations of the people's knowledge as a whole' (ibid.).

What I am proposing here is an Indigenous project that extends beyond voice or even perspective. One that embraces Indigenous Knowledges, which operate at several levels and cross cultural boundaries. Indigenous people share certain assumptions; when put together, these form an epistemological foundation and context. This paradigm is constructed as a collective core of interrelated assertions about Indigenous reality.

For my purposes, I define an Indigenous person as someone who (a) was born into lands with which she/he maintains an intimate and spiritual relationship; (b) belongs to a distinct linguistic cultural group; (c) has maintained a collective oral memory reaching as far back as the creation; (d) has unique customs and ceremonies that sustain her/his cultural survival and well-being; and (e) has maintained the view that Elders are the knowledge carriers and cultural historians. Indigenous methodologies have been summarized best by Marlene Brant Castellano (2000, 23): 'The knowledge valued in aboriginal societies derives from multiple sources, including traditional teachings, empirical observation, and revelation ... Aboriginal knowledge is said to be personal, oral, experiential, holistic, and conveyed in narrative or metaphorical language.'

So there are multiple sources of knowledge, and acknowledging this assisted my research with the Lubicon Cree. If an Indigenous discourse is to be developed, the community must be visibly present when researchers design and implement their studies. Indigenous people must be treated as more than 'collaborators.' They must be viewed as intellectual investigators and contributors. It is crucial that they be allowed the space and support to initiate an indigenous research agenda that will move forward the agenda of self-determination and nation building (Smith 1999). Battiste and Youngblood Henderson (2000, 44) continue to articulate the cultural approach to knowledge applied by Indigenous people. They argue that traditional ecological knowledge of Indigenous people is scientific, in the sense that it is empirical, experimental, and systematic. It differs in two important respects from Western science, however. Traditional ecological knowledge is highly localized and it is social. Its focus is the web of relationships between humans, animals, plants, natural forces, spirits, and land forms in a particular locality, as opposed to the discovery of universal laws.

Gregory Cajete coined the term 'ethnoscience' in *Look to the Mountain* (1994). He finds that Indigenous epistemology articulates the connectedness of Indigenous people to the land, the spiritual laws that govern that land, and how coexistence between animal, plant, and human life interrelate in a collective balance. He explores how ethnoscience reflects the uniqueness of place and is thus inherently tied to land and expressed through language and cultural practice. He states: 'Native community is about a "symbiotic" life in the context of a "symbolic" culture, which includes the natural world as a vital participant and co-creator of community' (2000, 95).

These authors have begun to construct an inclusive discourse for Indigenous research. The validity of Indigenous Knowledge is noted in Indigenous universal natural *law*, which posits that knowledge is spiritually based and ecologically derived. To remove the spiritual foundation of Indigenous Knowledge would be to destroy its very soul. Even colonial regimes were aware of that bare fact.

Indigenous peoples' justifications for their unique relationship to their natural environment are complicated (when not perilous). Indigenous people bring with them an ancient knowledge system that demonstrates their distinctive *form* of knowledge as well as its *dynamics* – that is, its capacity to recreate itself and resist Western hegemony. Indigenous people have long been misrepresented in the Western political structure – a misrepresentation viewed by many as a systematic rhetoric developed precisely in order to justify the oppression and genocide of Native 'others' (Jaimes 1992, 1–13). Maori scholar Linda Tuhiwai Smith (1999, 44) states that 'this sense of what the idea of the West represents is important ... because to a large extent theories about research are underpinned by a cultural system of classification and representation, by views about human nature, human morality and virtue, by conceptions of space and time, by conceptions of gender and race. Ideas about these things help determine what counts as real. Systems of classification and representation enable different traditions or fragments of traditions to be retrieved and reformulated in different contexts as discourses, and then to be played out in systems of power and domination, with real material consequences for colonized peoples.'

The relationship between theory and practice is a crucial one. In the pursuit of social justice, and based on their experience with malignant social realities arising from ill-informed colonial policies, Indigenous people have long been authorities on theory and practice. Many such theories resulted in practices that all but crushed the political power of an already marginalized people and that all but stopped cold their attempts to survive the ongoing exploitation of their lands and resources.

The Lubicon Cree are acutely aware of their position in the broader Canadian democratic process. 'Marginalization' does not quite capture their situation. Perhaps 'state terrorism' best describes the reality faced by their community. Indigenous peoples who live off the land were

long viewed as inferior, underdeveloped, and unworthy of preserva-
tion by Western institutions. Indigenous cultures and ways of life were
long ago given the death sentence (Brody 1981; Berkhofer 1979; Berger
1977, 1991; Coon Come, 1995). Indigenous peoples have lived off the
land for thousands of years and have faced the unthinkable – extinction. Before you wince, think that in Brazil alone, Latin America's larg-
est country, an average of one Indigenous group per year has been 'lost'
since 1900 – one-third of that country's original cultures. Renowned
anthropologist and Harvard-trained ethnobotanist Wade Davis (2000,
12–13) has written: 'Even as we lament the collapse of biological diversity, we pay too little heed to a parallel process of loss, the demise of cultural diversity, the erosion of what might be termed the ethnosphere,
the full complexity and complement of human potential as brought
into being by culture and adaptation since the dawn of consciousness ...
Worldwide, some 300 million people, roughly five per cent of the global
population, still retain a strong identity as members of an indigenous
culture, rooted in history and language, attached by myth and memory
to a particular place on the planet ... collectively represent[ing] over half
of the intellectual legacy of humanity.'

In the United States and Canada, there were at one time more than
sixty Indigenous languages; today, only four are expected to survive,
(ibid., 12; Wearne 1996, 9). Whether Indigenous cultures and their
knowledge will survive in North America depends in large part on
how willing the dominant society will be to value Indigenous people. If
the Lubicon Cree are any indicator of Canada's position on Indigenous
people's rights in this era of globalization, this country will be doing little more than documenting the extinction of one tribe after another and
watching history repeat itself. In North America alone, estimates of the
pre-contact population that reported a mere one million Indigenous
inhabitants have been proven fantastically wrong. The figure is closer
to 18 million, with fewer than half a million by the early 1900s as a
result of what is now often referred to as a campaign of genocide
(Jaimes 1992; Wearne 1996). It is doubtful whether North Americans are
prepared to accept any responsibility for the destruction of some 90 per
cent of the Indigenous population (Davis 2000).

According to Wesley-Esquimaux and Smolewski (2004), the Americas were colonized in three phases. The first of these they refer to as
'demographic collapse.' Citing estimates by Vecsey (1996) and Dobyns
(1983), they note that in 1492, 'an estimated ninety to one hundred and
twelve million Indigenous people lived on the American continent' and

that 'fifteen to eighteen million' lived in what is now the United States and Canada. They add that 'there is general agreement that mortality losses were staggering' (Esquimaux and Smolewski 2004, 12). Epidemics of smallpox throughout the Caribbean, Mexico, and Central America in the 1500s eradicated entire populations (ibid.). The arrival of smallpox in North America had a similar impact on Indigenous peoples. Waldram, Herring, and Young (in ibid., 9) examined Aboriginal peoples in Canada and noted that 'epidemics were not simply medical events but had far reaching consequences for Aboriginal societies ... In some cases, whole communities were decimated ... Among the survivors, the loss of significant numbers of community members altered leadership roles and disrupted the existing social structures.'

The smallpox pandemic was exacerbated by the frequency with which it recurred – every twelve to fourteen years, which left little time for populations to rebound: 'On the New Continent, while Indigenous people were trying to contend with never-ending waves of smallpox and influenza epidemics, they were also grappling with additional burdens of slavery, murder, colonialism and the indignity of being forcefully removed from their homes and traditional territories' (ibid., 26).

Indigenous and non-Indigenous scholars continue to debate the pre-contact population figures; meanwhile, the United States and Canada have yet to acknowledge the perpetration of a Native American Holocaust. Yet the figures point to no less. In the three centuries since contact with Europeans, the Indigenous population north of the Rio Grande has fallen 95 per cent (Jaimes 1992, 5–6). The history of Indigenous people in the Americas has yet to be told in full. Do children in Canadian schools learn about all the nations that have been wiped out since the European arrival, or about the extinction of entire populations? The Canadian judge Thomas Berger (1991, 13) has argued that according to 'European conquerors, the Indians had no story to tell ... [and] the images they portray [of the Indigenous population] go a long way towards explaining Spain's unwillingness – and ours – to accord Indians a meaningful place in the political firmament.'

According to Berger and others, then, Canada has followed the historical practice of failing to humanize Indigenous peoples and failing to see their value as peoples. Canada, like the United States, has nothing to be proud about in terms of its historical 'treatment of its Indians'; it has followed strategies and policies similar to those of other colonizers, and with similar outcomes. Berger suggests that if Indigenous self-determination is to be brought about, the first task must be to reveal the

Indigenous experience – an experience that has long been written out of colonial histories. The first task, in other words, is to establish that in Canada, some tribes were rendered extinct, and that genocide did occur and continues to occur. The Lubicon struggle for survival will provide proof of that.

The second phase of colonization, according to Esquimaux and Smolewski, was 'cultural dispossession,' which was characterized by negative social impacts, missionization, and assimilation. They cite Edward Said, who writes that 'the manifestation of colonialism is through the configurations of power. The political culture of colonial rulers operated within the frames of conquest, exploitation and repression to break existing social patterns and reassemble them according to European standards' (in Esquimaux and Smolewski 2004).

The Lubicon experienced both these phases. What is unique about their history is they passed through the two in rapid succession. The Spanish flu killed three-quarters of the Lubicon in the early 1900s. The Indian agents who visited them in 1934, just fifteen years after the epidemic, found that their population had fallen from roughly 2,500 to 200 (Goddard 1991).

The third phase of colonialism, according to Esquimaux and Smolewski, is 'cultural oppression,' which involves society's denial that anything unjust ever occurred. Such oppression, which flows from the systematic stripping away of Aboriginal people's identity, culture, and spirituality, has been institutionalized in Canada through Indian Affairs policy and carried out by agents such as the residential schools. The brutality of residential schooling has had a severe psychological impact on entire cultures and their communities (Esquimaux and Smolewski 2004; Duran and Duran 1995). Today, the Lubicon find themselves immersed in this last phase. The story of their struggle for survival – a story of historical trauma and psychological warfare – will unfold throughout this book. This research will examine how colonialism has operated in Canada historically and how it operates in the present day; it will also demonstrate that Indigenous Knowledge is a key source of power and resistance.

1 The 'Official Colonial' Lubicon History

Historical Overview

The Lubicon Cree are a hunting society in northern Alberta. For centuries – as far back as the Elders can say – they have lived around Lubicon Lake, hunting and trapping within a seventy-mile radius. According to James Smith (1987), the Lubicon and other Cree groups lived in the western territories long before the fur trade opened. Smith analysed the empirical, historical, ethnological, and linguistic data and found that the 'elders of the Lubicon Lake Band of bush Cree (saka*wiyiniwak), now at Little Buffalo Lake, Alberta, insist that they and their ancestors have always been in the region east of the Peace and west of the Wabasca rivers' (443). According to Elders, 'the Peace River has always been the boundary with the Dene-Tha branch of the Beaver Indians' (444). Smith cites Stevenson, an archaeologist who worked at Peace Point, in his finding that 'older informants of the community contend that Peace Point has been occupied for several hundred and, perhaps, thousands of years' (444). He goes on to state that the 'Beaver of the Dene-Tha Band confirm the Cree tradition. The Chief of the band ... asserted that all Beaver traditions hold that all raids by the Cree occurred west of the Peace River, in Beaver lands. According to him, the lands east of the Peace River were always Cree, while those lands west were Beaver' (ibid.). Their contact with outsiders was minimal, given their geographical isolation. It was not until 1954, when a mission school was built in Little Buffalo, that they learned the English language (Smith 1987; Asch 1985; Goddard 1991). Although the content of Smith's article, which described the land, seemed non-threatening, his anthropological observations of Lubicon social organization were of keen interest to the government. He described Lubicon social organization as 'bilateral cross-cousin marriage; a kinship system with Iroquois-type cousin terminology; classification of kin into consanguines and potential affines or in-laws and including temporary matrilocal post-marital residence with bride service; levirate and sororate formation of society into hunting groups ... local and regional bands; a "marriage universe" including the adjacent Loon Lake and Codotte Lake regional bands and a social identity reflecting the territory they exploited. There was recognition of government by consensus, especially as through heads of families guided by elders' (Smith 1987, 440).

As this story unfolds it will become apparent that the government in fact used Smith's 'marriage universe' to begin pulling the Lubicon membership apart by sending federal agents into Loon and Codotte Lakes to begin land claim negotiations. The dismantling of the Lubicon by requiring Lubicon members to join their relatives next door was just one tactic the Lubicon survived.

The Lubicon have been working towards a reserve settlement by legal means since 1939, and historically since the early 1900s (Edward Laboucon 1989, interview). They assert that during one of their Tea Dances, they were informed that in 1899 the government had signed a treaty with the other Cree. The Elders felt it was important for the Lubicon to secure their lands from the encroachment of white settlers (Smith 1988; Richardson 1989; Goddard 1991; Hill 1992). With the help of visiting missionaries, they wrote a letter to the Indian agency and sent delegates to Whitefish to speak with representatives concerning their taking treaty. A federal treaty with the Lubicon never materialized. Instead, the government 'signed up' a few Lubicon representatives to Treaty 8. The representatives the Lubicon sent to Whitefish did not quite grasp what had taken place there and turned to the missionaries for help in interpreting events (Goddard 1991).

While the Lubicon attempted to gain recognition as a distinct people, other events were influencing their actions, such as disease. A flu epidemic had devastated the area in 1916–18, reducing their population from 2,500 to about 200 (Smith 1987; Goddard 1991). Over the next several several decades, the Lubicon continued to lobby for an official agreement with the government. In 1939 they succeeded in gaining legal recognition as a band (Smith 1987; Lennerson 1988; Goddard 1991; Mandelbaum 1979).

The Lubicon described their early endeavours as reflecting their concerns about land encroachment. They attempted to protect their lands by contacting Indian agents in the area, and were visited by C.P. Schmidt, an Alberta agent. After visiting the Lubicon in August 1939, he reported: 'I was very much interested in this band and found them clean, well-dressed, healthy, bright and intelligent; in other words, people who want to live and do well' (Schmidt, in Goddard 1991).

Schmidt concluded that the Lubicon were a separate band between Lubicon and Buffalo Lakes. He calculated that 128 acres multiplied by 127 people would entitle the band to 25.4 square miles. An aerial survey was conducted, and by 1940 the reserve boundaries had been established (ibid.). At the time of legal recognition, the Lubicon had around 350 members, with three Metis families residing in their area. The reserve's size was agreed upon. However, because of the Second World War, there was a shortage of ground surveyors, so the actual ground survey never took place (ibid.).

In 1942 an official of the Department of Indian Affairs, Malcolm McCrimmon, removed well over one hundred Indians from the registered lists for northern Alberta, including ninety from the Lubicon lists. Having mutilated the band lists, he refused to acknowledge that the Lubicon were a band: 'If my recommendation is approved by the Minister, the number of Indians remaining on the membership list at Lubicon Lake would hardly warrant an establishment of a Reserve' (ibid. 26).

The mission boarding school was built in Little Buffalo, a small settlement occupied by L'Hirondelle, a fur trader who had married a Cree woman. He later lobbied for the school. The Lubicon did not favour a school in Little Buffalo; they wanted it to be nearer their settlement on Lubicon Lake. They wanted their children to learn English but were very unhappy about a year-round settlement in Little Buffalo (Goddard 1991). Most families were compelled to move to Little Buffalo if they wanted to live with or near their children (Fulton 1986; Smith 1987; Hill 1989). The mission school altered the social and economic structure from one based on seasonal migration to one that was sedentary and that relied on a cash economy. Most Lubicon, however, continued to rely on hunting and trapping income well into the 1980s. Bernard Ominayak remembers:

I was born in my parents' cabin at Lubicon Lake ... Life was like a cycle. In the fall, the men would hunt, trying to store as much food as possible for the winter. Then my dad would go up to his cabin at Bison Lake [70 miles north], trap for three or four weeks and come back with fur. My mother took the fur for drying, and my dad went out again. My mother, my brother and I were home alone most of the time. Then, as I got a little older, I got to go with my dad when he went hunting. If somebody shot a moose, he'd call the others over, and they would split it up between them. (Goddard 1985 55)

The Elders decided that the youth should learn English in order to pursue the group's land claim. Thus, Walter Whitehead and Bernard and Larry Ominayak were persuaded by Elders to attend high school in Grouard.

In Grouard, Walter met Harold Cardinal, who would later help the Isolated Communities Board (which consisted of Northern community representatives) deal with various land claims. Walter was the first elected Lubicon chief, in the early 1970s. It was he who began to lay the legal groundwork for the land claim. His first task was to conduct a census to establish Lubicon membership. He regularly attended meetings of the Isolated Communities Board, which was presided over by William Beaver (Whitehead 1989, interview). Oil exploration began in the area at about the same time. The provincial government began to build an all-weather road into the area to facilitate oil exploitation (Asch 1986; Goddard 1991).

Walter Whitehead, working with the Alberta Indian Association, attempted to file a caveat with the Alberta Land Registration Office. The caveat was the first legal notice the Lubicon registered with the government. The province's response was to refuse to file the caveat. The Alberta Indian Association helped the Lubicon file suit against the province for refusing to file their caveat. The Lubicon then sought federal assistance in pursuing their case with the province. The Lubicon were informed that the federal government was the 'trustee' of Indians; later, they learned that the federal government would indeed be involving itself in the case – on behalf of the provincial government (Lennerson 1989; Goddard 1991). According to the UN International Covenant Civil and Political Rights (ICCPR) Communication No. 167/1984, the sequence of court proceedings was as follows:

3.3 On 27 October 1975, the Band's representatives filed with the registrar of the Alberta (Provincial) land Registration District a request for a caveat, which would give notice to all parties dealing with the caveat land of their assertion of aboriginal title, a procedure foreseen in the Provincial Land Title Act. The Supreme Court of Alberta received arguments on behalf of the Provincial Government, contesting the caveat, and on behalf of the Lubicon Lake band. On 7 September 1976, the provincial Attorney General filed an application for a postponement, pending resolution of a similar case; the application was granted. On 25 March 1977, however, the Attorney General introduced in the provincial legislature an amendment to the Land Title Act precluding the filing of the caveats; the amendment was passed and made retroactive to 13 January 1975, thus predating the filing of the caveat involving the Lubicon Lake Band. Consequently, the Supreme Court hearing was dismissed as moot.

3.4 On 25 April 1980, the members of the Band filed an action in the Federal Court of Canada, requesting a declaratory judgment concerning their rights to their land, its use, and the benefits of its natural resources. The claim was dismissed on jurisdictional grounds against the provincial government and all energy corporations except one (Petro-Canada). The claim with the federal government and Petro-Canada as defendants was allowed to stand.

3.5 On 16 February 1982, an action was filed in the Court of Queen's Bench of Alberta requesting an interim injunction to halt development in the area until issues raised by the Band's land and natural resource claims were settled. The main purpose of the interim injunction, the author states, was to prevent the Alberta government and the oil companies ('the defendants') from further destroying the traditional hunting and trapping territory of the Lubicon Lake People. This would have permitted the Band members to continue to hunt and trap for their livelihood and subsistence as part of their aboriginal way of life. The Provincial court did not render its decision for almost two years, during which time oil and gas development continued, along with rapid destruction of the Band's economic base. On 17 November 1983, the request for an interim injunction was denied and the Band, although financially destitute, was subsequently held liable for all court costs and attorneys' fees associated with the action. (Human Rights Committee 1990, Thirty-eighth session, 3)

While the Lubicon were pressing their claims through the courts, several significant events took place. Walter Whitehead resigned as chief and Bernard Ominayak was elected to that office. The Lubicon started to organize their band office and receive funding for band administration. They hired a consultant, Fred Lennerson, who served as their adviser. The late Harold Cardinal, a Cree, recommended lawyer James O'Reilly to represent the Lubicon land claim.

From 1974 through 1985, the Lubicon became increasingly dependent on welfare. According to band records, only 9 per cent of members were receiving social assistance in 1981. By 1985, 95 per cent were receiving assistance (Fulton 1986; Goddard 1991).

Another significant event was the completion of a road through Little Buffalo in 1978. By 1980 at least ten major oil companies were present on Lubicon land and had drilled more than four hundred wells (Asch 1986; Goddard 1991). Michael Asch (1986, 8) summarized the negative impact that oil and gas development had on the region's wildlife and its habitants. Using the band's own statistics, he found that there had been a 'significant decline in the economic productivity': 'income from trapping has declined from per capita average of over $5000 in 1979 to under $400 in 1984–85 and ... moose production has declined from 200 for the band in 1979 to just 19 in 1984–85. At the same time, the percentage of people receiving welfare has risen from just under 10 per cent of the population in 1979 to over 95 per cent in 1984–85.'

The band reported a marked increase in social breakdown at this point. Ominayak would later describe a community in stress:

> The change in diet, influx of outsiders brought our health down. The T.B. outbreak in the eighties was just the first sign that development was having an impact on our health. There are no sure studies to show exactly the kind of impact. However, we have witnessed a marked increase in alcohol consumption, violence and even suicide. We never had these social problems before. All the development, welfare, nothing to do, nothing to hunt, changed our traditional structure of men having pride in providing for their families. I'll never forget the day my father gave in and signed for welfare, I'll never forget that moment. He held out, but in the end had to ask for assistance. Babies are sick, many don't make it, just look at our graveyards. You'll never measure the impact, not in economic, social, environmental, emotional, psychological, cultural or spiritual areas. Science can't measure that, only we can. And I can tell you, it's devastated us. (Bernard Ominayak interview 1991)

While the community was experiencing these rapid developments, its political leaders engaged in a media campaign to bring attention to the plight of the Lubicon. In 1983 the Lubicon appealed to the World Council of Churches in Vancouver. After investigating, the council sent a letter to Prime Minister Pierre Trudeau. Dr Anwar Barkat wrote. 'In the last couple of years, the Alberta Provincial Government and dozens of multi-national oil companies have taken actions which could have genocidal consequences' (Barkat in Goddard 1986, 86).

The province pursued its own campaign by trying to declare Little Buffalo a provincial hamlet. In 1981 the official status of Little Buffalo was changed from 'Indian Settlement' to 'Provincial Hamlet.' This meant that all the laws applicable to hamlets were now also applicable to Little Buffalo. Members of the Lubicon band were now subject to municipal and school taxes. Tax notices were sent out to members, and the residents of Little Buffalo were required to apply for land tenure or a land lease. Those who did not comply with these requirements were threatened with fines and/or demolition orders (Fulton 1986; Goddard 1985, 1991).

In 1984 the Department of Indian Affairs accepted that the Lubicon Lake Band should enjoy mineral rights, and that they should be provided with funds to create a variety of programs and with the tools to protect their traditional lifestyle of hunting and trapping. Also, the federal Justice Department determined that the Lubicon were legally entitled to a reserve (Asch 1986; Goddard 1985). In November 1984 the federal Minister of Indian Affairs, David Crombie, announced that former justice minister David Fulton had been appointed to mediate the case, which now involved Ottawa, the province of Alberta, and the Lubicon. Fulton undertook a year-long study and forwarded his recommendations to all three parties in February 1986; two days later, he was 'excused' (Goddard 1991). Fulton's recommendations, which favoured the Lubicon, were ignored by Parliament (Fulton, in *Lubicon Settlement Commission of Review Final Report* 1986).

With the help of their adviser, Fred Lennerson, the Lubicon launched a boycott of the 1988 Winter Olympics in Calgary. This action brought considerable national and international attention to their land claim. They had succeeded in raising awareness of their situation, but they had yet to succeed in negotiating an agreement with the federal government.

Ottawa responded to the boycott by deferring the matter to the courts. The Minister of Indian Affairs, Bill McKnight, proposed that a forum be established where the band's grievances could be addressed (Goddard 1991; *Lubicon Settlement Commission of Review* 1993). In the coming months, discussions failed over who would mediate the 'grievances.' The Lubicon withdrew from the federal court proceedings in

1988, stating that the only reason they had involved themselves in the first place was to force the Canadian government to obey its own laws. Having withdrawn from the courts, the Lubicon declared that the band was taking jurisdiction over its traditional territory, effective 15 October 1988. The federal government responded by cancelling the mediation process, arguing that the 'assertion of jurisdiction precludes any opportunity for negotiations or discussion' (Goddard 1991). On 15 October 1988, after failed discussions with the province and the federal government, the Lubicon erected a road blockade. On 20 October 1988, armed RCMP officers arrested twenty-seven Lubicon and their supporters, including two Quakers and two (West) Germans.

Two days later, the Lubicon met with Premier Donald Getty of Alberta and arrived at an agreement with him, now known as the Grimshaw Accord. Getty allowed for seventy-nine square miles to be transferred to the federal government for the purpose of establishing a Lubicon reserve; a further sixteen square miles would be under Lubicon jurisdiction. The seventy-nine square miles were to include subsurface and surface rights, as at other reserves in Alberta; however, the extra sixteen would include only surface rights (Grimshaw Accord 1988). The federal government agreed to accept the seventy-nine-square mile reserve, as well as the extra sixteen, but was prepared to provide services only to members it considered 'Indians.' McKnight was prepared to recognize 235 of the approximately 500 Lubicon as Indians (Lennerson 1989; Goddard 1991). Band membership turned out to be a case issue in the long months of discussions that followed with the federal government. In the end, the Lubicon were not prepared to allow Ottawa to divide the band on the basis of status.

Negotiations between Ottawa and the Lubicon carried on into the new year. Besides membership, there were many other unresolved items on the agenda. In January 1989 the federal government offered a take-it-or-leave-it deal that would provide the band with no more than $45 million. The Lubicon reviewed the offer and found that it contained few of the self-sustaining provisions for which they had been negotiating. There were also problematic clauses in the fine print – for example, one such clause contained a final release of all legal rights:

48.7 In consideration of the rights and benefits provided by this offer, the Band and such persons who are entitled to adhere to Treaty No. 8, through the Chief and Council of the Band:
   (a) will cede, release and surrender to Her Majesty in Right of Canada

(i) all their aboriginal claims, rights, titles and interest, if any, in and to lands and waters anywhere within Canada, and;

(ii) all their claims, rights or causes of (legal) action whether collective or individual which they ever had, now have, or may hereafter have, or arising out of or by reason of Treaty 8, save hereafter specifically provided;

(iii) all their claims, rights or causes of (legal) action whether collective or individual which they ever had or now have as alleged in [legal actions filed by the Lubicon people];

(iv) all their claims, rights or causes of legal action they ever had, now have or may hereafter have under, or arising out of or by reason of any Imperial or Canadian legislation or Order-in-Council or other action of the Government-in-Council or Canada in relation to Metis or half-breed scrip or money for scrip. (Department of Indian Affairs, Lubicon Settlement Offer 1989)

By accepting the take-it-or-leave-it offer, the Lubicon would have been giving up the right to sue for further compensation. So they rejected that offer, arguing that it was clearly prejudicial to Lubicon rights to sue for compensation (Goddard 1991).

In February 1988 the provincial announced that the Diashowa pulp mill would be built near Peace River; this involved the granting of a timber lease of 11,000 square miles, including 4,000 square miles of traditional Lubicon territory (Goddard 1991; *Lubicon Settlement Commission Review, Final Report* 1993). Obviously, this mattered a great deal to the Lubicon. At the time, McKnight, besides being Indian Affairs minister, was responsible for the Western Diversification Fund, through which he was pumping millions of dollars into the infrastructure for the pulp mill. Clearly, this was a conflict of interest for McKnight, who was supposed to be settling the land dispute at the same time. McKnight was aware that the province had negotiated the lease of Lubicon lands to forestry companies.

In February 1989 in Edmonton, a series of meetings were held between Lubicon band members and government representatives. These individuals were interested in exercising a clause in Treaty 8 that provided for land to be held in severalty. According to the treaty, such land was for families who wished to live apart from the band. Lubicon leaders were informed by reporters that a dissident band was organizing itself. Chief Ominayak decided to call an early election to demonstrate that he was representing the mandate given him by the Lubicon people. He also hoped to demonstrate that the Lubicon were a nation, notwithstanding the government's contention that many Lubicon had signed up to join the Woodland Cree. The chief and his council were re-elected (Goddard 1990). The dissident group was formally referred to as the Woodland Cree. Shortly afterwards, its members secured a land base around Cadotte Lake.

As far as the Lubicon were concerned, the point of this initiative was to undermine their land claim by establishing a band that would 'harvest' their members and thereby render their land claims moot. The federal government had been utilizing this strategy for decades, as far back as the days of Malcolm McCrimmon in the 1930s (Ominayak 1991, interview).

The dissidents recruited members by promising them $1,000 for each family member if they would sign with the Woodland Cree. I personally spoke with members who had received this offer, and they were unaware that the money they would receive for signing up would later be deducted from their welfare cheques (field note, 1991). Journalist John Goddard was in the community to report on the voting for the Woodland Cree land deal. He investigated the story and found that people were being given a monetary incentive to sign; not only that, but each member who signed up would be paid $50 simply for voting.

By 1992 the Woodland Cree had struck a land claims deal. About sixty former Lubicon had signed up with the new band, according to Lubicon band records. The Lubicon were confident that the government had failed to recruit enough of their members to substantially alter the land claims negotiations. They were quick to point out that the high birth rate among the Lubicon would soon compensate for lost members (Bernard Ominayak 1992 interviews).

According to Lubicon residing at Loon Lake, the federal government had been lobbying for them to sign up with another government-created band, the 'Loon Lake Band' (ibid.). It is possible the lawyers who engineered the Woodland Cree and Loon Lake bands found their blueprint in the work of a joint federal band genealogy study conducted in the early 1980s. It seems the federal and provincial governments were aware of the 'marriage universe' as delineated by James Smith (1987). Whatever the case, both were working hard to persuade Lubicon to join the Cadotte and Loon Lake communities cited by Smith. The government was actively recruiting people who were known to be dissatisfied with the Lubicon leadership owing to kinship differences.

Meanwhile, the UN Human Rights Committee rendered its decision on 26 March 1990. The Lubicon learned of its release on 27 April and reviewed it on 1 May. That committee found Canada in violation of Article 27 'so long as historical inequities ... and certain more recent developments [continue] to threaten the way of life and culture of Lubicon people' (International Covenant on Civil and Political Rights, Human Rights Committee 1990, 38th session, 29).

In Canada, an independent, non-partisan commission was established in 1991 to seek a resolution to the Lubicon land claim. This twelve-member commission included a lawyer, anthropologist Michael Asch, and the president of the Alberta Federation of Labour. After a year-long investigation it released its findings to the public in March 1993. The *Lubicon Settlement Commission of Review Final Report* stated:

Our principal finding is that the governments have not acted in good faith. They have:

a) Passed retroactive legislation to undermine legal claims,

b) Appropriated royalties that, had a reserve been established at an appropriate time, would have been in Lubicon hands, and

c) been in conflict of interest because they act as interested party, beneficiary of royalties, and presumed judge of the validity of Lubicon claims... .

We feel that there is in-built conflict of interest within the mandate of the Minister of Indian Affairs and Northern Affairs. On the one hand he is to protect the interest of the Indian people; on the other hand he is put in a situation where he is to make decisions regarding the development on contested lands, decisions with negative consequences for Indian peoples. A case in point: Minister Bill McKnight, responsible for Western Diversification Funding, allowed funds for development by Diashowa on disputed Lubicon lands. We found the Lubicon have acted in good faith in negotiations. Having heard Chief Ominayak's report regarding deliberate avoidance of oil wells in the selection of their land, Commission members acknowledge the Lubicon's sincere efforts to facilitate resolutions. The Lubicon want open and public negotiations, and have responded to invitations from the governments to negotiate. They have presented a well thought-out plan for a settlement, to which they still await an adequate government response. They have also agreed to the process of mediation ... We agree with E. Davie Fulton who said: 'I cannot see this being a precedent because this is an entirely unique set of circumstances. Never before in our history – and let's hope never again – has a situation existed where a Band was promised, over 50 years ago, a settlement and a reserve that would have given them a livelihood, set them up in that way so that they wouldn't have suffered so dreadfully from the loss of their forms of livelihood and they would other benefits from it – promises which have not been fulfilled, which have been stymied, which have been met with obfuscation and difficulties by the very people responsible for implementing the promise ... So a generous settlement recognizing the equity of the situation could not possibly serve as a precedent for other settlements, because there's no other such situation.'

Various bodies continue to condemn Canada for stonewalling the Lubicon land claim; meanwhile, the community itself has been under unbearable pressure. The social impact, according to Bernard Ominayak, has been immeasurable.

In the next section of this chapter, I outline the field research I undertook for this book between October 1989 and June 1993. This section is important, because it describes the devastation suffered by the Lubicon as well as their cultural survival and resistance. Lost in the official Lubicon history are the Lubicon people themselves – their beliefs, values, culture, and spirituality. In my retelling of the Lubicon story, I will insist that the Lubicon world – a world of breathtaking cultural beauty, integrity, and distinctiveness – is the only legitimate context for this research.

Indigenous Self-Determination and Indigenous Theory and Method

Recent work on Indigenous peoples has shown that when engaging with issues such as self-determination and Aboriginal social justice, an analytical framework is imperative. The Cree of Quebec have demonstrated that Indigenous peoples living off the land do have power – enough power to stop huge corporations and governments from destroying their land and people. Canadian and multinational stakeholders now realize that Indigenous peoples are not passive recipients of development and globalization. History has shown us that Indigenous peoples define their rights and defend their identities based on traditional laws and knowledge.

Issues such as resistance, cultural survival, and ethnocentrism are relevant to analyses of the colonial process and its impact on Indigenous cultures and rights; yet such analyses hold little value for Indigenous peoples. In other words, the knowledge that we Indigenous scholars must so painfully and diplomatically demonstrate to our aca-

Matthew Coon Come and Ovide Mercredi. Assembly of First Nations hosting the Lubicon in Ottawa, 1992.

demic audience is common knowledge in Aboriginal communities. We have to prove oppression to these people, even though for us it is a lived experience. What is important to the colonized is usually not important to the colonizers, and the two sides often have opposing agendas that influence the funding of research. The challenge before us is to write 'Indians' in – not, however as mere victims, but rather in a way that values Indigenous (in this case Lubicon) knowledge. The logic of this book's structure is beholden to both worlds. Western academic knowledge and Indigenous Lubicon knowledge need not be at odds with each other; indeed, there is space for each to compliment the other.

The rich cultural tapestry of the Lubicon world requires a negotiation of appropriate positions of authority and space so that its contributions can be fully appreciated. Theory and methodology are critical when it comes to framing the Lubicon struggle and demonstrating that their construction of their own reality has as much validity as the 'scholarly stuff.' For too long, Indigenous people have been positioned as objects for examination and as subjects/informants for Western intellectuals. Their representation by the West has been as a backdrop for Western theories. Worse yet, Elders and others have been exploited for their knowledge and reduced to poetic anecdotes and as footnotes for the central scientific figure, the non-Native hero – that is, the person who actually has something important to say. I discussed this at length with Bernard Ominayak, the Lubicon chief.

To simply package my Lubicon research as another 'land claim' story and to depict their struggle as merely a tragic story would not encourage Canadians to interrogate their own assumptions about Indigenous peoples, about hunting peoples, about Indigenous struggles for their land, and (importantly) about their acceptance of and passivity towards injustice. I want to go beyond the legal, economic, and technocratic jargon of modern land claim representations, and in order to do that, I need to present the present struggle within an Indigenous framework that is sensitive to the unique assumptions and positions of the Lubicon. And finally, I want to make a statement about Indigenous Knowledge and Power. I want to show how culture and heritage shape Indigenous people's psyches and spiritual groundings and offer strength through a sense of 'knowing.' Audiences, be they Indigenous or non-Indigenous, must be urged to *act* on the injustice that the Canadian government has inflicted on this small group of Cree.

This undertaking demands that I explain Indigenous Knowledge and methodology. My hope is that this explanation will heighten interest in the Lubicon struggle and encourage people to learn about the Lubicon, about the injustices they have faced, and take part in social action for justice.

The story of the Lubicon struggle can be transformed by Indigenous theory and methodology. This approach represents the Lubicon within a framework that positions their knowledge and experiences as informed, valid, and authoritative rather than subjective, unscientific, biased, and politically charged. The Lubicon instructed me to 'do whatever you feel you have to in order to get as many people as possible educated to our situation, and hopefully pressure the government to be fair and just in their dealings with us' (Bernard Ominayak, 2000, interview). The motivation for exploring Indigenous thought, theory, and methodology is to help bring about self-determination, and my call for the Indigenous situation to be represented within a sound systematic Indigenous epistemological foundation is part of that project. Learning about this small Indigenous community in northern Alberta and its struggle against encroachment by multinational corporations and governments will begin, as one Elder put it, with 'a long journey of the mind.'

Little Buffalo, Alberta. Photograph by Tom Hill, Woodland Cultural Centre, 1992.

The Scholarly Stuff

In this section, I explore three areas. First, I examine emerging issues in the work of contemporary scholars writing on Indigenous theory and method. Second, I investigate literature about resistance and re-examine ethnocentrism as it is encountered in analyses of resistance. This discussion is key to the project of decolonizing social-scientific inquiry. Third and finally, I will articulate the Lubicon struggle for survival in the words of the Lubicon themselves. In the present climate of state-sponsored ecological and political terrorism, there is a need to construct an authoritative space for the Lubicon people to articulate their experiences. Indigenist pedagogical inquiry requires that we develop a structure of Indigenous Knowledge in which oral tradition is the main source of Indigenous methodology.

Admittedly, the scope of this text is limited, in that I cannot draw clear conclusions about broader government intentions or the Western canon of knowledge. I can, however – and this is more important – raise questions about Canada's integrity as a democratic state, a state that often admonishes its southern neighbour for its aggression and injustice towards oil-rich countries in the Middle East. During the Second Iraq War of 1993, the Americans' 'shock and awe' bombing campaign was evening entertainment for the West, and brought most North Americans ever closer to completely desensitizing themselves to the sight of brown-skinned people dying. Yet hidden from view are those policies in which state-sponsored terror is rooted – the very policies that exact human suffering. The Lubicon are distinguished by their oil-rich lands from those Indigenous groups which have none; like the Colombians, the Iraqis, and others, they have been cursed with the presence of black gold in their yards. What few people in the West understand is the lengths that Western governments are willing to go to maintain control of oil – at the cost of lives, if necessary. Noam Chomsky (2003, 60) argues that 'like many other centers of turmoil and state terror, Colombia is part of an important oil producing region, and a significant producer itself; much of the same is true for Chechnya, Western China.' He discusses how the fumigation of poppy fields – an act that kills peasant and Indigenous children and that displaces thousands of others – is yet another example of the West's unethical foreign policies, which ensure that its interests are met at the expense of 'others.' The Lubicon are Indigenous members of the global village, whose sole 'crime' is that they are sitting on large oil deposits. In the West's new world order, this combination is enough to render them political, economic, and even moral pariahs. Developing an Indigenous framework is an act of resistance to this Western hegemony; it is an act of survival. The Lubicon, like leaders from Six Nations, often declare their empathy for people of the Middle East, South America, and other places with violent and repressive regimes (Elders Summit 2004).

The contribution developed by and with the Lubicon in this book is intended to add to a universal body of Indigenous theory and method that already exists. Throughout this book, the Lubicon themselves will articulate an alternative approach, one that challenges Western ways of knowing. In doing so, they will show clearly that the structure of Indigenous Knowledge can be an empowering tool for all Indigenous peoples.

Colonialism is often the backdrop for Indigenous people's stories, but do people really know what colonialism in Canada is?

What is colonialism? Frideres and Gadacz (2005, 4–7) contend that there are seven component of Canadian colonialism:

The incursion of the colonizing group into a geographical area is closely followed by destructive effects on the social and cultural structures of Indigenous groups. The colonizers destroy the people's political, economic, kinship, and (in most cases) religious systems. A related condition of external political control and Aboriginal dependence is then legislated. For Canada's Indigenous peoples, external control is organized through the Department of Indian Affairs and Northern Development, which is also responsible for cementing Aboriginal economic dependence. Colonization includes the provision of poor quality social services for the colonized, especially in the areas of education and health. Two more components of colonization relate to the social interactions between Aboriginal people and colonizers. Colonialism is fuelled by racism – that is, a belief in the genetic or cultural superiority of the colonizer and the inferiority of the colonized. And lastly, Indigenous people are prevented from entering into the mainstream economy – one of the most debilitating components of colonialism for Aboriginal people.

In Canada, the Indian Act has created and continues to encourage a 'culture of poverty' among Aboriginal people by establishing two economies – one for Canadians who have the skills required for employment, and one for Native people who do not possess those skills (ibid., 2005). I would add as a Mohawk that when we do work hard to do well, the state often declares our activities to be illegal. You know what I am talking about here – our tobacco fields. Perhaps we are next in line for fumigation policies. Needless to say, whether it is Mi'kmaq being shot at for fishing in Burnt Church, New Brunswick, or Mohawks selling cigarettes, economic engagement by Native people often involves dangerous conflict with the state and often ends in prison terms. While I was completing this book, Six Nations took a stand and occupied land claimed by us that had been sold to private developers. In April, May, and June of 2006, I stood at the barricades along Highway 6 watching non-Native people from Caledonia, Ontario, scream racist epithets while we stood silent, stunned at the hate emanating from the mob. For us this was about land illegally taken, for Caledonia's citizens and their mayor, Marie Trainer, it was about inciting hatred. Publicly, she made comments that Six Nations members interpreted as labelling them as welfare recipients. In an appearance on CBC NewsWorld earlier in the day, the mayor said that 'residents of the town were being hurt economically by the protest and don't have money coming in automatically every month ... [The Indians] needed to know what the people of Caledonia thought. I have to stick up for my people just like they're sticking up for themselves.' The NewsWorld report of that day continued: 'The incidents [of that day] marked a further deterioration in relations between the protesters and town residents following a noisy confrontation at the barricades Monday night that led to the arrest of one person' (http://www.cbc.ca/story/canada/national/2006/04/25/caledonia-protest-060425.html). The Caledonia Citizens Alliance orchestrated confrontations where mobs broke through police lines and attacked our people, who were pepper sprayed. It was a scene that played out colonialism in all its forms and displayed its deep roots in racism.

The media did little to present any factual, historical information – a failure that led to Hollywoodized representations of 'Indians' terrorizing innocent white people for no reason. Incidents in which of Elders and women were Tasered while sharpshooters surrounded the occupation site were barely noted. It is almost normal for Indigenous people to have guns pointed at them wherever they protest injustice. Never mind the historical truth of the situation, which was clearly articulated in a press release by a number of esteemed academics and scholars at McMaster University on 25 May 2006:

> The Haldimand Proclamation of October 25, 1784 granted to the Six Nations Confederacy six miles of land on each side of the Grand River, from its headwaters to the mouth on Lake Erie. That legacy has shrunk to a small percentage of its original size in the intervening period. Six Nations lands today comprise less than 4.8 per cent of that which was promised in the Haldimand Deed of 1784 (reduced from approximately 950,000 acres to approximately 45,000 acres today). The Six Nations Confederacy has actively sought over a long period, and with little success, to recover its lands. Since 1974, 29 claims have been filed by Six Nations, only one of which has been fully resolved, in 1980. The Hamilton-Port Dover Plank Road claim, which includes Douglas Creek, was filed in June 1987, long before the current conflict. More recently, with regard to the Henco development at Douglas Creek, several months before the blockade first started Six Nations people and supporters organized a public information session at Douglas Creek to draw attention to the fact that the development was taking place on land over which Six Nations claimed ownership.

> We hope that civic leaders will speak out against any occurrence of bigotry, especially given the long period of peaceful cohabitation between Six Nations and Caledonia residents. While the root causes of the conflict must be addressed, we applaud the recent demonstrations of good will and good sense by those in the Caledonia community who have joined

those in the Six Nations to de-escalate the confrontation. We also applaud the federal and provincial governments for agreeing to negotiate with the Confederacy Chiefs and Clan Mothers, the form of government outlined in the Great Law of Peace and in place with the Haudenosaunee people since before contact with European colonizers. This Confederacy was brutally repressed by the federal government when the Royal Canadian Mounted Police invaded Six Nations territory in 1924. We urge that this good will be nourished and supported by everyone in Canada concerned for justice.

[signed] Dr Daniel Coleman, English and Cultural Studies; Dr Wil Coleman, Political Science and Institute on Globalization; Dr Harnish Jain, School of Business; Dr Graeme MacQueen, Religious Studies; Dr Joanna Santa Barbara, Peace Studies; Dr George Sorger, Biology; Dr Mark Vorobej, Peace Studies and Philosophy; Dr Gary Warner, French; Dr Don Wells, Labour Studies and Political Science.

The state has used force to silence Indigenous people for more than a century. The consequences of standing up for land rights can have severe impacts, as seen by Six Nations people and the Lubicon. The state finds it crucial to repress Indigenous peoples' land rights by maintaining control over their resources. Only in this way can it continue its colonial practices.

Indigenous people have always been coerced into dependency. One result has been that a body of dominant research continues to plague Indigenous people by treating their knowledge as invalid, mythological, and inferior in its scientific capacity (Persky 1998). Cree legal scholar Sharon Venne (1998, 161) contends that the UN and universities are key agencies for developing social justice: 'One of the significant aspects of the UN Working Group on Indigenous Peoples is that it has become the forum for Indigenous Peoples to meet yearly to share the situations in their territories. It is also an opportunity to form joint strategies in key areas ... These initiatives help to educate state societies so that they can put pressure on their governments to recognize the rights of Indigenous Peoples.' Scholarly networks also facilitate dialogue between nation-states and Indigenous peoples. Because resources and space are lacking that would support the development of Indigenous self-determination or thought, an 'Indigenous paradigm' does not exist. The field of Indigenous scholarly work is very young, yet it is exciting that now, in this era, we are finally able to develop a global network. Indigenous people are finding it inspiring that people can be so alike regarding their epistemologies, cultural and social constructs, philosophies, and political ideologies yet continue to remain so different from their colonizing counterparts. For the states themselves, this is a threat; recently, Canada and the United States refused to sign the UN Declaration on the Rights of Indigenous Peoples. Sylvain Larocque (2006), in an article for Canadian Press, wrote:

> Canada has teamed with the United States and Australia to stop the United Nations from passing a declaration on the rights of indigenous peoples, says Amnesty International. The human rights group, along with opposition parties, accused the Conservative government of Prime Minister Stephen Harper on Monday of stalling the declaration along with these other nations. It's been twenty years that the international community has been working on a declaration on aboriginal rights, said Alex Neve, secretary general of Amnesty International Canada.
>
> 'It's difficult to imagine an important issue of human rights that the governments of the world have taken more time to resolve,' Neve said Monday.
>
> 'The problem of the human rights of indigenous peoples is urgent,' said Angus Toulouse, president of the Assembly of First Nations. 'It's not necessary for the rights of these people to come in second place in order to please the United States, New Zealand and Australia.' Last month, representatives of those three countries sent out a joint statement calling the declaration 'profoundly imperfect.'
>
> The UN declaration would guarantee 'auto-determination' for indigenous peoples, giving them the right to reclaim traditional territory and refuse military activity upon traditional lands. Indian Affairs Minister Jim Prentice said the declaration contravenes the Canadian Charter of Rights and Freedoms, when it comes to aboriginal land claims, as well as federal laws on national defence.

The UN has been a forum for colonialist dialogue; it has done little to ease the human suffering of Indigenous peoples.

Indigenous ideology is not a product of colonialism, but a revelation grounded in ancient teachings about Creation and our inherent responsibilities and rights. Creation stories often frame our assumptions about the world, and this knowledge evolves over time. Throughout the processes of resistance to colonization and the pursuit of self-determination, Indigenous discourse relies on original teachings as its terms of reference. These narratives are rooted in original and evolving stories that have fuelled and will continue to fuel Indigenous resistance to the hegemony of the West, as well as allow Indigenous cultures to thrive and evolve.

Indigenous People Dismantling Western Claims to Power: Decolonization

The legal approach to defining Indigenous rights, argues Venne (1998, 1–3), rests in the world view of the West. Customary international law erases the legal value of peoples who do not share this world view. Venne concludes that colonial powers are a common threat to Indigenous peoples' cultural survival. Similarly, Patricia Monture-Angus (1999) argues that the West has used its own legal framework as a tool to dispossess and exploit Aboriginal people and to deny them their rights. In sum, the Western rule of law is not a tool for liberation, nor is it one for self-determination. Taiaiake Alfred (1999, 43) explains: 'One of the major differences between the Western and Indigenous conceptions of power and justice is that the cultural values that determine fairness in the Western conception are limited (with a few rare exceptions) to human society. Among Indigenous people, the cultural framework used to determine whether or not power is used appropriately includes not only human social relationships but all other relationships as well.'

Alfred focuses on the conceptual framework necessary to explore positions of authority, determine frames of reference, and bring together the knowledge of Indigenous peoples. All of this is required to validate an emerging Indigenous paradigm.

The key to self-determination is nested in Indigenous constructions of knowledge, laws, and institutions. The restructuring of traditional institutions in a modern setting is only one strategy for achieving self-determination, and one that the Lubicon have adopted quite deliberately as a source of empowerment. The Lubicon paradigm is embedded in processes they themselves have encouraged.

The need for a critical discourse on Indigenous issues such as protection of lands is of paramount importance if there is ever to be a dialogue between Indigenous peoples and state governments. There is a discourse that has developed from early legal decisions about Indigenous rights, and it suggests that Europeans have their own land claims and that Indigenous nations must therefore negotiate with Crown authorities. Judge John Marshall wrote in 1830: 'The Indian nations had always been considered as distinct, independent political communities, retaining their original rights, as the undisputed possessors of the soil, from time immemorial ... The words "treaty" and "nation" are words of our own language, selected in our diplomatic and legislative proceedings, by ourselves, having each a definite and well understood meaning. We have applied them to Indians, as we have applied them to the other nations of the earth' (in Berger 1991, 80).

The idea that Indigenous peoples now have land claims is at every level absurd. Modern land claims are testimony to the government's ability to develop discourses, which result eventually in legal policies that undermine Indigenous sovereignty. The Haudenosaunee people have a documented history of resisting efforts by Canadian and American governments to colonize them. The Haudenosaunee view the Lubicon position as an ongoing assertion of the same spirit of autonomy that our ancestors asserted.

In 1923, Haudenosaunee Chief Deskaheh travelled to Geneva to speak to the League of Nations and defend the right of his people to live under their own laws, on their own land, and under their own faith. He was not allowed to speak, and he was prevented from returning home. He died in exile. Even so, his vision nourished the generations that followed.

A few months before his death in 1925, Chief Deskaheh made his last speech, over the radio, from Rochester, New York:

This is the story of the Mohawks, the story of the Oneidas, of the Cayugas – I am a Cayuga – of the Onondagas, the Senecas, and the Tuscaroras. They are the Iroquois. Tell it to those who have not been listening. Maybe I will be stopped from telling it. But if I am prevented from telling it over, as I hope I do, the story will not be lost. I have already told it to thousands of listeners in Europe. It has gone into the records where your children can find it when I may be dead or be in jail for daring to tell the truth. I have told this story in Switzerland. They have free speech in little Switzerland. One can tell the truth over there in public, even if it is uncomfortable for some great people.

This story comes straight from Deskaheh, one of the chiefs of the Cayugas. I am the speaker of the Council of the Six Nations, the oldest League of Nations now existing. It was founded by Hiawatha. It is a League which is still alive and intends, as best it can, to defend the rights of the Iroquois to live under their own laws in their own little countries now left to them, to worship their Great Spirit in their own way, and to enjoy the rights which are as surely theirs as the white man's rights are his own.

The Haudenosaunee have constantly lobbied worldwide for support in resisting the imposition of the Indian Act and the theft of their lands. They have legally maintained their argument within the same framework of reference as Deskaheh.

The United Nations and Amnesty International have taken decisions on the Lubicon case. In a public report, Amnesty International cited the UN Human Rights Committee and reaffirmed their position. It states: 'In March 1990, the United Nations Human Rights Committee (UNHRC) concluded that "historical inequities" and "more recent developments" have endangered the way of life and the culture of the Lubicon Cree. The Committee ruled that "so long as they continue" these threats are a violation of the Lubicon's fundamental human rights.'

In 1987 the UNHRC agreed to examine the case because the Lubicon no longer had any recourse through Canadian courts that would address the threats to their culture and livelihoods in a timely and effective manner. In view of the seriousness of the Lubicon's allegations that they were on the verge of extinction, the UNHRC asked Canada 'to take interim measures of protection to avoid irreparable damage' to the Lubicon Cree while the UNHRC considered whether the Lubicon's rights under the International Covenant on Civil and Political Rights (ICCPR) were being violated. Amnesty International believes that the rights of Indigenous peoples already recognized in international law, treaties with the Crown, the Canadian Constitution, and rulings of Canadian courts and in other aspects of Canadian law are an essential part of the framework of protecting and promoting human rights in Canada. Therefore Amnesty International calls on all levels of government in Canada to uphold and promote all rights of Indigenous peoples, rather than seek ways to diminish, extinguish, undermine, or circumvent these rights. Amnesty International also calls on the Canadian government, like all governments, to uphold its commitments to core international human rights conventions, to live up to widely agreed-upon human rights standards, and to comply without delay and in a broad and systematic fashion with the urgent recommendations of its own commissions and UN treaty monitoring bodies.

This recommendation was then echoed by the UNHRC, which, when reviewing Canada's compliance with the ICCPR in 1999, urged 'decisive and urgent action be taken towards the full implementation of the RCAP recommendations on land and resource allocation.' The UNHRC also recommended that Canada's policy of requiring extinguishment of inherent or Aboriginal rights be abandoned because it violates Canada's human rights obligations under the ICCPR (AMR:20/01/2003, Amnesty International).

Canada continues to ignore pleas from Indigenous people, the UN, and international bodies such as Amnesty International. The challenge here for Native people is to learn from experience and remain active participants in dismantling colonialism in real terms. While I was writing this book, Six Nations land claims exploded onto the national scene. Several women – Dawn Smith, Janie Jamieson, and Cheyanne Williams – lobbied the Confederacy to stop a housing subdivision from being built in Caledonia, Ontario. Months of negotiations led nowhere. Finally, in November 2006, our traditional government released its position to the public. It states:

> The council of the Chiefs of the Haudenosaunee, Grand River Territory, wish to affirm and clarify our land rights in the tract confirmed by Governor Frederick Haldimand on October 25, 1784. In making this statement, the Council of Chiefs wants to make it clear that we hold certain land ethics and principles that must be respected in any arrangements on land use or occupation. The Haudenosaunee, and its governing authority, have inherited the rights to land from time immemorial. Land is a birthright, essential to the expression of our culture.
>
> With these land rights come specific responsibilities that have been defined by our law, from our Creation Story, the Original Instructions, the Kaianeren:kowa (Great Law of Peace) and Kariwiio (Good Message). Land is envisioned as Sewatokwa'tshera't, (the Dish with One Spoon); this means that we can all take from the land what we need to feed, house and care for our families, but we also must assure that the land remains healthy enough to provide for the coming generations. Land is meant to be shared amoung and by the people and with the other parts of the web of life. It is not meant for personal empire building.
>
> First and foremost is the concept that we are connected to the land in a spiritual way. The earth is our mother and she provides for our long term well-being, provided that we continue to honor her and give thanks for what she has provided.
>
> We Haudenosaunee have upheld our tradition of giving thanks through ceremony, and in the cultural practices that manifest our beliefs, values, traditions and laws. Planting, cultivating, harvesting, gathering,

hunting, and fishing also have spiritual aspects that must be respected and perpetuated if the land is to provide for our future generations, and the future generations of our neighbors. We are stewards. Our spiritual obligation is part of that stewardship.

Second, according to our law, the land is not private property that can be owned by any individual. In our worldview, land is a collective right. It is held in common, for the benefit of all. The land is actually a sacred trust put in our care, for the sake of the coming generations. We must protect the land. We must draw strength and healing from the land. If an individual, family, or clan has the exclusive right to use and occupy land, they also have a stewardship responsibility to respect and join in the community's right to protect the land from abuse.

We have a duty to utilize the land in certain ways that advance our Original Instructions. All must take responsibility for the health of our Mother.

Our ancestors faced overwhelming odds and relentless pressure to give up our lands. We all know that unscrupulous measures were employed to seduce our ancestors into selling the land. At other times, outright fraud took place, as was acknowledged in the Royal Proclamation of 1763. The agreements we recognize reflect an intention to share land, and to lease land, within the context of the Covenant Chain relationship that our nations maintain with the Crown.

In any land issues, we want it understood that the following principles will govern any actions taken by the Haundenosaunee Council of Chiefs of the Grand River Territory.

1) The land is sacred to us. It defines our identities, belief system, languages and way of life.
2) We hold the Aboriginal and treaty title to our lands collectively.
3) Our treaty relationship with the Crown is still alive and in force and directs our conduct in our relationship with Canada. Within this relationship, in terms of the treaties continue to bind both our government and the Crown.
4) We require a careful accounting for the Brown's dealing with our lands, and the return of any lands that were improperly or illegally taken from our ancestors.
5) We require an accounting for the funds administered or held by the Crown for the Six Nations people, and restitution for any funds unaccounted for.
6) It is not only within the context of our treaty relationship with the

Crown that we see justification for such accounting and restitution. Canadian and international law is clear on the right of Haundenos-aunee to seek justice on these matters.

7) In any agreements with the Crown concerning land our goal is to promote and protect a viable economy for our people on our land – an economy that will be culturally appropriate, environmentally sustainable, and not injurious to our people and our neighbors.

8) Our fundamental approach is that Six Nations lands will come under the jurisdiction, management and control of Six Nations people. The federal and provincial governments must not impose juris-dictional, policing, taxation, and/or economic activities as part of land rights settlement.

Our people, our laws, and our government have survived being thought-ful, respectful, diligent and practical. In our relations with the Crown, and in any negotiations concerning land and the resolution of land related issues, we will continue to apply those principles.

What can the discourses of Indigenous people teach us with regard to the relations with non-Natives? The struggles of the Lubicon Cree and the Haudenosaunee for their land base and rights demonstrates clearly Canada's unwillingness to exercise its own laws and apply them equally to all citizens (World Council of Churches, in Goddard 1991, 87; Martin-Hill, 1995; Dickason, 1992, 390–2; York and Pindera, 1992, 253–7). The legal case of the Lubicon also demonstrates the state's ongoing pressure to extinguish Aboriginal title in lieu of settling land claims. The Canadian government's policy of forcing Aboriginal people to bar-ter away their rights in order to have the opportunity to achieve basic social justice is just one way in which the government exploits and vio-lates Indigenous rights.

The Lubicon Cree continue to face social and economic assaults on their traditional way of life. Morbidity and mortality rates have increased owing to state-sponsored development policies and the gov-ernment's profound reluctance to resolve their land claims. In 2004, Rainy Jobin, a Lubicon spokesperson, attended the Six Nations–hosted International Indigenous Elders Summit. He told the summit that according to his band's own records, in one year, out of twenty-one pregnancies, only three reached full term. Yet the human costs of the Lubicon land claim were being hidden from the Canadian people. One would be hard pressed to find similar miscarriage rates anywhere else in the world. The environmental degradation and rapid pace of development the Lubicon must contend with amount to nothing short of environmental terrorism, and the impact on the Lubicon people's health has been disastrous. Chief Bernard Ominayak has described the human costs of development and political marginalization:

> That is an added burden to the overall problem that exists, when you have a people that are faced with resource development. Really no way, or limited knowledge, as to how to defend themselves in the so-called political system that is in place. Or the legal system that's not in place by the government of Canada. So, when you have a group of people that when you're doing business, that feel that everyone is honest, at both sides of the table, where we were raised to respect all people and all forms of life, whether it be animal or any of the trees, all these things. So, it's a hard lesson that we have had to learn through this process, whereby we found out the white man doesn't care. All they're after is money and how to make more money, with no regard to the land or animals or any life. Anything that gets in their way they want to push aside to make way for the modern, or so-called modern, technology that benefits them. (Martin-Hill 1995, 103)

In 1983, Dr Anwar Barket of the World Council of Churches echoed the chief's sentiments: 'In the last couple of years, the Alberta Provincial Government and dozens of multi-national oil companies have taken actions which could have genocidal consequences.' Put differently, the Alberta government has yet to settle the Lubicon land claim or slow down development on the band's traditional lands (Martin-Hill 1995, 77; Goddard 1991, 86). International trade agreements such as NAFTA are exacerbating the problem pointed out by Barket and Chief Ominayak, and on an a national scale. According to Perez (1998), 'The signing of the NAFTA agreement between Mexico, Canada and the USA was the final blow, the one that forced the elders of the Mayan communities to declare war on Mexico. The EZLN called this agreement a "death sentence." As a prerequisite to Mexico being invited into NAFTA, Canada and the USA also demanded the abolition of article 27 of the Mexican Constitution, which after the Mexican Revolution of 1910, protected Native lands.'

The tactic of removing legal protection from Indigenous lands at the behest of foreign corporate interests is also being practised by the Canadian state, Diashowa being one example. The millions being pumped into oil and gas development on Lubicon lands will continue to generate conflict until meaningful dialogue is established.

Indigenous Peoples' Voices

Trinh Minh Ha (1989, 59) writes:

> But once more, *they* spoke. *They* decide who is 'racism-free or anti-colonial,' and they seriously think they can go on formulating criteria for us, telling us where and how to detect what they seem to know better than us: racism and colonialism. Natives must be taught in order to be anti-colonist and de-Westernized; they are, indeed, in this world of inequity ... Whatever the issue, they are trapped in a circular dance where they always find themselves a pace behind the white saviors.

Indigenous people make assumptions about social reality and value systems. These assumptions are immersed in their spiritual relationship with the natural world. They have a tradition of ideas that, when brought together, reflect a common adherence to the Creator's natural law (Alfred 1999, 4; Hill 1992, 63). This Indigenism, as Taiaiake Alfred explains (1999, 88), amounts to a recognition by Indigenous people that they share a collective ideology: 'Indigenism brings together words, ideas and symbols from different Indigenous cultures to serve as tools for those involved in asserting nationhood. It does not, however, supplant the localized cultures of individual communities. Indigenism is an important means of confronting the state in that it provides a unifying vocabulary and basis for collective action. But it is entirely dependent on the maintenance of the integrity of the traditional Indigenous cultures and communities from which it draws strength.'

The late John Mohawk, a Seneca scholar, described the development of the Iroquois Great Law, which established a confederacy with the principle of peace as its foundation. The Peacemaker, one of the Haudenosaunee's greatest philosophers, convinced the five nations embroiled in war that clear thinking would lead to peace and power. He persuaded the people that the greatest gifts given to humans – their minds, their hearts, and their communication skills – would overcome the tradition of rule-through-fear. The Haudenosaunee Enlightenment took place at about the same time the Europeans were developing their conquistador thinking (Barreiro 1992, 25). The concepts developed by the Haudenosaunee demonstrate that an evolved *consciousness* existed prior to the arrival of Europeans. They also illustrate how the philosophy of the Peacemaker promoted strength through unity (Wright 1992, 223–38; Lyons and Mohawk 1992, 1–13). According to Basic Call to Consciousness (Akwasasne Notes 2005), Indigenous people are connected by a common philosophy that has always fuelled resistance to oppression. Indigenous people share common bonds related to a *collective* colonial experience, as well as a belief system based on an all-empowering *consciousness and rationality.* Spirituality is central to the epistemological foundations of Indigenous societies. Their ceremonies are vehicles for reproducing and reaffirming Indigenous ideologies and identities.

The Indigenous societies of North America share specific cosmological constructions regarding their relationship with the universe. The universal principles encompassed by Indigenous ideologies include the understanding that human beings are endowed with neither the right to dominate others nor the right to destroy that which is around them. The belief that every life form has a spirit and should be acknowledged as necessary to human sustenance is in direct conflict with Western notions of man dominating nature. An Indigenist epistemology involves the humanization and subjectification of not only people, but animals, plant life, rocks, and all of Creation. This is not 'mythology,' or even religion; it is a universal principle at the core of Indigenous consciousness. The cosmological 'awareness' of Indigenous peoples is complex in that it accounts not only for this world but also for the principles governing the spirit world. These ways of knowing involve a *developed* sense that can inform behaviour and influence social action as outlined in the Great Law (Akwasasne Notes 2005; Castellano 2000)

To be powerless is to not even know who you are; to be weak is to display disrespect and ignorance. The claim of Western culture to an objective rationality is perceived by Indigenous scholars as one of the greatest myths constructed by Western scholars. The arrogance bound within claims to objectivity by social scientists leads only to hollow understandings of 'others.' All humans are cultural constructs. Science itself emerged in resistance to Western religious world views. The linear view of the world stands in direct contrast to the holistic view of the world held by Indigenous people. The cyclical and comprehensive multidimensional Indigenous epistemology accounts for the dynamics of coexistence and interrelationships. Progress and development are not logical concepts in the circular model. The past, present, and future inform everyday actions, including political, social, economic, and spiritual spheres, which are related to the whole (Cajete 2000; Deloria 1992).

The notion that human behaviour is shaped solely by economic or political issues is foreign, if not absurd, to Indigenous peoples.

The core manifestations of Indigenous ideology take place in the ceremonial context. Through ceremonies, ideas and beliefs emerge, which are reinforced through physical and spiritual actors. The cultural expressions of Indigenous thought are diverse, but the assumptions and principles are similar. Each sphere of the circle – the social system, the economy, the political structure – is fuelled by the spiritual centre. For example, the potlatch of the Northwest Coast peoples is central to their spiritual, political, economic, and social life.

In a holistic framework, time and space are collapsed. Events of the past can be important in everyday discourse and integrated with what happened yesterday or the day before. This intimate relationship with history is a social fact, and many tribal peoples map the future by reciting events of long ago. This circular time frame moves distances in a manner that is foreign to Westerners. Space is aligned with the movement of time. Indigenous Knowledge intertwines all cosmological relationships, the earth, the stars, and the universe. The kinship system is based in the cosmos with the earth as mother, the moon as grandmother, the sun as a father or uncle, and so on. The idea of compartmentalizing temporal space according to property or commodities is a foreign concept for many Indigenous peoples, one that conflicts with the spiritual values that shape Indigenous consciousness (Deloria 1994, 99).

Resistance to colonial forces is not a reaction to colonial domination; rather, it is often an expression of sacred knowledge that is non-negotiable because it was given to the people by the Creator. The strength of Indigenous 'power' through ceremonies was known to the colonizers, as evidenced by their repeated attempts to wipe out these practices. In Canada, the potlatch, the Sun Dance, the Ghost Dance, and many other ceremonies were outlawed by the Indian Act in 1914 and made punishable by prison. This law was not repealed until 1951, and it was only in 1978 that the United States allowed ceremonies to be practised openly (Cummins and Steckley 2001; Jaimes 1992, 17). Elders often refer to ceremonies as a source of knowledge, in much the same way that Western scholars refer to their 'classical' literature.

For many tribal groups, the right to live off the land and practise 'a way of life' is the central inherent right they are seeking to protect. Indigenous Knowledge is transmitted through oral processes; indeed, Indigenous peoples have long participated in an ongoing dialogue. The experiential nature of Indigenous Knowledge has fostered a rich and all-encompassing sense of the understanding *process*. Individuals who are recognized as 'Elders' and thus as 'wise and experienced' are respected by their communities. So it should be no surprise at all that the Lubicon have chosen to spend their energies in ceremonial activities instead of wholeheartedly engaging in Western legal arenas that deny their knowledge and that serve only to disempower them and dispossess them of their inherent rights.

In their worst moments, when policies of physical and cultural genocide were being followed, the Lubicon resisted this repression by embracing their traditional ideologies, which are woven tightly into their contemporary setting. As Indigenous Elders and scholars point out, their movement has been strengthened by the ability they have acquired to communicate and utilize dominant discourses to articulate their own representations and reconstructions. But the challenge for Indigenous people is still great. As long as Indigenous cultures continue to be sacrificed in the name of progress, development, and industrialization, they will remain in the trenches fighting for survival.

The task of recreating Indigenous identities and recasting traditional values as modern discourse is hardly new. The way in which Indigenous research and discourse is being constructed has several implications for social justice. As Maori scholar Linda Smith (1999, 189) states: 'Reconciling market-driven, competitive and entrepreneurial research, which positions New Zealand internationally, with the need for Maori to carry out research which recovers histories, reclaims lands and resources and restores justice, hardly seems possible. This is precisely why debates around self-determination and the Treaty of Waitangi have been significant. The attempt by Maori to engage in the activities of the state through the mechanism of the Treaty of Waitangi has won some space in which Maori can argue for different sorts of research priorities.'

The emerging Indigenous discourse is based in values and world views that attempt to uphold egalitarian ethics. The idea of *authority* and *position* must be addressed when Indigenous discourses are developed. In this project, respect and honesty are crucial. We must conduct our research with integrity and – even more important – *collectively with others*.

The hierarchy that is inherent in European and Western social science has placed the primitive/Native at the 'low' end of the Western measuring stick and the civilized/Westerner at the 'high' end (Hill 1995, 39-40). While the Native peoples of North America shared their concepts with Europeans, Europeans appropriated not only Native lands and resources but also their knowledge and cultural heritage, which is now woven tightly into Western culture. The historical (and continuing) oppression of North America's Indigenous peoples has taken many forms: the appropriation of Indigenous cultures, the decimation of Indigenous populations through disease and warfare, the heavy exploitation of the natural resources, the forced relocation of entire nations, assimilation policies, and the appropriation of Indigenous culture and knowledge (Weatherford 1988, 1; Barreiro 1992, 7–27; Berkhofer 1979, 20). It is imperative that Indigenous peoples reclaim their knowledge and histories as an act of decolonization. While Canada continues to entrench and legalize ethnocentrism through various court decisions (Persky 1998, 1–21), Indigenous people continue their efforts to assert those Indigenous rights which are embedded in Indigenous knowledge (RCAP 1997, 525).

It must be remembered that, as powerful as the West's economic forces are, Canada's assimilation policy has *failed*. History has shown us that Indigenous people have actively subverted and undermined policies designed to strip them of their language, culture, spirituality, and knowledge. State agencies and missionaries have failed in their bid to 'continue until there is not a single Indian left in the body politic' (Titley 1986, 72).

Assimilation as a policy has failed miserably; but as a practice, its impacts are still very much part of the Indigenous experience (RCAP 1997, 2). Ovide Mercredi, former National Chief of the Assembly of First Nations, has noted that 'we are dealing with the impacts of the federal policies as a collective, many have adopted a learned behavior of loss of authority, this happened when the parents brought their children to the shores and allowed them to take their children away, and the children asked, "Why didn't you fight them?" Allowing them to decide for us is a form of internalized colonialism, and it will take some time to undo the colonial behaviors and mindsets. It takes time to gain confidence and assert our authority over our lives once again.'

There is a great deal of confusion and dysfunction within Indigenous communities. Healing is central to the process of self-determination and the business of reconstructing, rebuilding, reinventing, and revitalizing Indigenous nations. If we continue to try to validate ourselves to the very people who almost destroyed us, we will only remain in a colonial mindset. This is contrary to our goals. We must position ourselves in the centre of our own territory, instead of speaking from their margins to tell them about us. We must learn to take ownership of ourselves and of our own truths.

Methodology of Reciprocity

Indigenous communities are leery of researchers as a consequence of their past experiences with research (L. Smith 1999). For many national Native organizations such as the National Aboriginal Health Organization and the Institute of Aboriginal Peoples' Health, ethics have become an important topic of discussion. These organizations encourage researchers, governments, and academics to collectively discuss issues surrounding ethics – issues such as 'confidentiality,' 'who benefits,' 'imposing agendas,' and 'ownership of data.' These discussions validate and restate the concerns that Elders and leaders involved in this study have raised regarding how research should be conducted in Indigenous communities.

Regarding my research for this book, the Lubicon and I agreed to several key points initially: they would own all the material I collected during my research; they would benefit directly from my field research; they would be involved in developing the research project; and they would control the release of the information I gathered. Also, no information from the field research would be released or published without the Band Council's consent, all the people I interviewed would have a chance to review their transcripts and withdraw or edit their interviews, and the Lubicon would have the right to declare some material confidential and refuse to release it. In this vein, Battiste and Youngblood Henderson (2000, 140) have written:

> The council [Canadian Research Council Policy Statement of Ethical Conduct on Research on Human Subjects] considered it a good practice for researchers to respect the culture, traditions, and knowledge of the Aboriginal group; to conceptualize and conduct research in partnership with the Aboriginal group; to consult members of the group who have relevant expertise; to involve the group in the design of the project; to examine how the research may be shaped to address the needs and concerns of the group; and to make the best efforts to ensure that the emphasis of the research, and the ways chosen to conduct it, respect the many viewpoints of different segments of the group in question.

The Lubicon emphasized that if the research might cause harm or create problems for the community, it should not be published. Their approval for this book's publication was not given to me until 2000. I do not know why it took so long; perhaps the Lubicon feared that the government might use its findings against them in the courts, or use it to fragment the community.

The ethics surrounding confidentiality posed another challenge to this research. According to the Tri-Council Policy on Research Ethics, the 'subjects' must normally remain anonymous. This posed a problem, in that no one I interviewed desired anonymity. In fact, the chief and the community members thought it important for me to highlight their kinship affiliations, to help people understand why they refused settlements that would have given status to one band member and not another.

The only person whose identity I have withheld in this study is not Lubicon. He is the Confederacy Chief and Elder who assisted with my field research. He has since passed away. Strained relations with his daughter led to uneasiness on my part about releasing his name, so I have not; but it is sad that the soul of this work has been denied identity. All of those who loved him know his name; for those who don't, I will call him Henry Joe.

The Lubicon and other Indigenous people often perceive anonymity as dehumanizing. So they often felt slighted or insulted when I offered confidentiality, and told me they *wanted* to be identified. In fact, few Indigenous people I have ever interviewed have agreed to remain anonymous. A Faithkeeper from Six Nations once asked me, 'Why can you have a name and identity and I cannot?'

A lot of past research has reduced Indigenous people to objects and dehumanized them to the point that they cannot recognize themselves. Today, part of Indigenous resistance is to speak and represent self, with no 'expert' Eurocentric analysis and authority. So the Lubicon emphatically rejected being anonymous in this study. One Lubicon woman told me, 'You mean they won't know who is speaking? What is the point if my children don't know it was me speaking, you could just go make it all up!' Everyone involved agreed that their identities would indeed be made known.

A key question asked today regarding research about Indigenous people is 'Who benefits?' For this project, the answer was clear from the start: the Lubicon would benefit. As Linda Smith has put it, Indigenous research agendas must have an Indigenous social justice agenda. Unless the community will benefit in some direct way, there is no point to conducting Indigenous research. The Lubicon did more than just collaborate in this research; they *controlled* the research. The researcher would benefit (by the requirements for a PhD), but so would the Lubicon, who determined how the research would be conducted in their community. As I will discuss later, their plans were quite complex, as well as significant to the exploration of Indigenous Knowledge.

Sorting Out the Sacred

An understanding of community dynamics is vital to the success of collaborative research. It is a challenge to understand the role that ceremonies play in Indigenous culture, but by omitting ceremonies from the research, I would have been omitting the ideological centre of Lubicon existence. According to Battiste and Youngblood Henderson (2000, 140), 'access to sacred knowledge is ordinarily restricted to particular individuals ... This can pose two kinds of problems for researchers. No single individual can ever be aware of all the cultural concerns that may exist in the community; a broad process of consultation with different groups and elders may be needed before determining whether a site, object, or design is important. In addition, the necessary information may be confidential, such that it cannot be revealed completely to outsiders, or even to the rest of the community.'

I had to confront these challenges while researching with the Lubicon. To help in this process, a Haudenosaunee traditional leader accompanied me to Little Buffalo, Alberta. This indirectly positioned the researcher as a 'traditionalist to the community.' The presence of the Elder and the Indigenous Knowledge he held brought a sense of dignity and integrity to the research conducted in the Lubicon community. This was not a calculated move on my part; rather, it was an heartfelt attempt to link the Lubicon struggle to the Haudenosaunee Confederacy in a much broader project of mutual networking and support. It is interesting to see how Six Nations land claims are tied to the Lubicon; I have often wondered whether the media or the people who occupied the site near Caledonia are even aware of the strong connection between the Lubicon and Haudenosaunee.

I relied heavily on Henry Joe for guidance when it came to interpreting experiences in a manner that would not jeopardize the 'sacred.' He foresaw events that I couldn't even imagine at the time.

Henry also explained several times that I should remain quiet and follow their lead. He warned me not to walk in front of the Lubicon, since it was they who knew the land. It took quite a while for me to comprehend what Henry was trying to explain, but I eventually did. For my research to succeed, I would have to understand that this was their land and that the spirits of their ancestors or guides resided in certain places. There are places that are sacred to them, and it took time for me to learn where not to tread. By not paying attention to such matters, I would have been disrespecting the Lubicon and their spirits.

My research on Lubicon spirituality and ceremony has placed some of this book on sensitive ground. I made repeated attempts to learn the protocol from the Lubicon Elders, ceremonialists, and medicine people. However, 'straight answers' from Elders are not part of Indigenous pedagogy; rather, these answers come through observing, listening, and learning. Having entered the community as a Mohawk woman conducting research, I encountered a vast array of experiences that probably would not have arisen had there not been an 'Indigenous comradeship' – or to borrow from Taiaiake Alfred (1999), 'Indigenism.' I do not deny that other anthropologists have experienced bonding of some sort – be it emotional, spiritual, or intellectual – with an Indigenous people or community. I am, however, saying that the experience of being an Indigenous person with a membership in my own community led to two Nations interrelating at the ceremonial level, the level of the sacred. This led to countless hours of agonizing over what to include in this book and what was to be excluded as 'sacred.' But the Lubicon trusted me to follow my own conscience and teachings.

Collective Research: Enter the Mohawk

The collective nation-to-nation nature of this project and my identity as an Indigenous researcher have shaped this book – both its design and its content. Indigenism forged a common identity between Lubicon and Haudenosaunee and created, for a time, an alliance rather than an academic collaboration. This is not a racial or essentialist statement. A century of assimilation policies has detached many Indigenous people from their culture, identity, heritage, and spirituality. The position I present here is that Indigenous Knowledge is acquired through learning and through life experience. When I began this project, I was just beginning to learn about my culture, my heritage, and what it means to be a Mohawk woman today.

By participating in Lubicon ceremonies I learned that it was within these sacred spaces that the Lubicon sought political guidance. During those ceremonies, strategies were discussed and collective decisions were made. The intimacy of the ceremonies facilitated a collective bond that nurtured relationship building and trust among all. The development of trust between the Six Nations Confederacy and the Lubicon Nation provided the dynamic for the research. Through the sacred space, the Lubicon shared their deep and rich knowledge, which would later provide the core for this work. Nation-to-nation exchanges and relationships were affirmed formally through kinship systems. Six Nations and Lubicon leaders' relationships were intertwined spiritually, and this informed the directions they would take politically. Thus, the research could not be separated from community dynamics; rather, it was interwoven in meaningful ways for everyone involved.

For the purposes of the academic research agenda, I adopted a somewhat contrived dialogue to represent the Western understanding of field research, which is often referred to as 'collaborative or participatory research.' I had to adopt this dialogue in order to justify this work to the research team and university. Utilizing an Indigenous framework, the Lubicon positioned my family within a kinship system, and this led to a number of reciprocal interactions and obligations.

The research conformed in many ways to what was expected by the university; even so, meaningful dialogue took place in Indigenous spaces that did not conform to conventional Western research. A decade later, I am just beginning to understand the weight of Lubicon grief over the devastation of their land and the permanent loss of their way of life, to which they were profoundly tied. And all the while, we are asking them to participate in some research meeting in Montreal to talk 'research designs'!

In 1991 the Lubicon political leadership wanted to organize the Lubicon women into an active group. Chief Ominayak was concerned over the possible imprisonment of his entire band council, and he wanted the women to be more politically active. For this purpose, the work of this project expanded to organizing political and spiritual gatherings and attending ceremonies and meetings with government officials. This work, though, evades being classified as 'advocacy anthropology.' What happened, rather, was that understanding and respect for Elders and leaders created a reciprocal obligation that shaped my research interactions with Lubicon and even Six Nations people. The methodology of reciprocity included integrating Lubicon goals with the project – even if those goals might fall outside the project's 'official' agenda. Accountability to the community meant taking on extra work, including holding information meetings about the Lubicon in my own community to gain the support of the Six Nations Confederacy's leadership and community for the Lubicon's contemporary struggle. Many meetings between the Six Nations Confederacy and the Lubicon were held in both communities. The development of a relationship between the Haudenosaunee Confederacy and the Lubicon added a new dimension to my research with the latter. The Confederacy responded by assigning me tasks such as organizing meetings, creating and disseminating written information, making travel arrangements, raising funds, and liaising between the two nations. My role as a Mohawk usurped my role as researcher, or so it appeared at the time. Forging a link with the Haudenosaunee Confederacy became the Lubicon leadership's overriding interest in my research project. I carried out my assigned responsibilities with a great deal of trepidation, since they raised questions about my motives within my own community (or they just thought I was nuts). Learning Haudenosaunee protocols, and mediating this work in whatever manner was culturally appropriate for the two cultures thus also became part of the broader project. I had not been born into a traditional family, so it was easy for me to land myself in hot water with some Clanmothers and others who felt that the research had no place within the Confederacy. I must admit they had a point: the cost of developing a methodology of reciprocity seemed high. On the other hand, the relationships established by those involved, the networks they developed, and the common experiences and Traditional Knowledge they shared were worth every single uncomfortable moment.

Canadians do not seem to understand that for many, ignorance about Indigenous culture and heritage is the norm today. Even more frustrating is that the society that is now disappointed with our 'un-Indianness' is the very same one that made my mother ashamed of her Indianness; either way, we continue to be made to feel inferior and ashamed. That is our reality.

As for the demands of being a student of both institutional and traditional knowledge, well, it can drive one a bit crazy. Being tested by both worlds is a pressure unknown to many. To refer to the methodology of this project as 'applied,' 'advocacy,' or 'participatory' would be inaccurate. It can only be described as a methodology of reciprocity.

The relationship of reciprocity is not unique to this project. In fact, throughout history, Indigenous communities have transformed fur traders, anthropologists, and others into kin affiliates. It is the Indigenous way. The Lubicon desired to have Haudenosaunee leaders – both Clanmothers and chiefs – support the community by attending Round Dances, Tea Dances, and court hearings. These interactions nurtured a

sharing of world views on the environment, sovereignty, and spirituality; they also provided important moral support. The conversations
that I collected as data could not possibly have taken place had Haudenosaunee leaders not been present in Little Buffalo. A natural flow of
knowledge and exchange of information occurred, demonstrating how
much alike the two groups were as well as how different. It was a privilege to be exposed to such a wealth of Indigenous Knowledge. Both Six
Nations and the Lubicon became heavily involved in the research
whenever and wherever they could, and their assistance is much
appreciated.

The methodology of reciprocity requires the researcher to be account-
able to the community, to develop research methods within a reciprocal
relationship, and to ask the crucial question, 'Who is going to benefit
from this research?' If a community is unable to see itself as the direct
beneficiary of the project, it is not a methodology of reciprocity. If a
community is not part of the research design and the research itself, the
project is not using a methodology of reciprocity. Furthermore, for the
research collected to embrace the principles of that, it must be at the
very least the shared property of the community. Lastly, the community
must agree to the release of the findings in any publications arising
from the research, even if this conflicts with the researcher's agenda, as
it did in this instance.

Data Collection

The community decided that participatory research was appropriate
both for their purposes and for those of the project. My first interviews
were with the political leaders, since they were comfortable articulating
their views to the public and did not mind tape recordings or videos.
The open-ended questions flowed from various events that were
unfolding 'in the field,' such as the development of a new band, the
Woodland Cree, and the Mohawk stand-off at Oka. I did not formally
approach the community members until I had spent several months in
the community and a certain level of trust had been established. Sometimes these were not formal interviews; rather, I made journal entries
after a ceremony during which we had shared our deepest thoughts,
fears, and feelings. Field experiences sometimes indirectly affected my
friendships or interactions; such experiences, though, had no place in
the research, as confidentiality had to be respected. The pain felt by the
Lubicon is not up for consumption by the very society that created the

circumstances in which they are suffering. The voices of the Lubicon in the pages that follow have been transcribed directly from audio tapes. The interviews are structured according to the Lubicon kinship system.

The Interviewing Stage

Interviews have their own dynamics; it is not simply about researchers collecting interviews with subjects. Long before being interviewed, the subjects themselves interview the researcher. On arrival in any community, a complete stranger is always a bit suspect. Wade Davis (2001, 27) explains this eloquently: 'As a young anthropologist I never understood how I was supposed to turn up at some village – perhaps of the Barasana, a people of the Anaconda, who believed that their ancestors had come up the Milk River of the Amazon from the east only to be disgorged from the belly of the snake onto the banks of the upper affluent– and announce that I was staying for a year, and then notify the headman that he and his people were to feed and house me while I studied their lives. If someone that intrusive appeared on our doorsteps, we would call the police.' The notion that researchers have the right to impose themselves on a community demonstrates that anthropology is saddled with a lens of arrogance. How the researcher becomes involved in a community has a strong impact on any project.

This project began in 1988, when the Lubicon presented an inspiring lecture at McMaster University sponsored by the Peace Studies program. The Lubicon Elder and chief were asked if there was anything that could be done to help them; they replied that they needed a great deal of help. At that moment, I began my MA in sociology; I also began to develop a relationship with the Lubicon leaders. The Lubicon agreed to participate in my project in part because of their strengthening relationship with the Confederacy. In fact, I decided to pursue this project and a PhD in part because the Lubicon hoped to maintain their relationship with the Confederacy – a relationship that had begun during my fieldwork. It seemed that my graduate work might serve as a means for the two nations to stay involved with each other.

My earliest research consisted of conversations with the Lubicon and their advisers. Being in the community was a whole other experience. Like Davis, I often felt like an intrusive, obnoxious invader during the field research. The community members questioned my project's motives. They would ask, 'Why are you here?' and 'What do you want from us?' Elders inquired about my background and knowledge and watched how I conducted myself. After a period of observation, some members accepted me but just as many stayed aloof. This is the 'interviewing stage' with the researcher as subject.

The Lubicon Are Not Informants

The Lubicon always understood that they were the guides and authorities for this project. The Elders and the community governed the research, and they knew it; it followed from this that I was a guest in their lives. Because I did not impose an agenda external to the project, and because I understood where the boundaries were, a level of trust developed over several years. The best approach to research is to learn from your hosts, tailor your research to support their agenda, and wait for an appropriate time to introduce your interests. The Elder who travelled with me many times to visit the Lubicon advised me, 'Never walk ahead of them, they will take care of you but don't nose around, listen, have patience and you'll learn' (Henry Joe interview 1989). He also suggested that I wait for the host to invite us instead of assuming that we were invited. Indigenous protocols are determined by simple respect. Davis's comments summarize well how important it is for researchers not to impose on their hosts. You wait until you're invited in – that is Indigenous protocol. Gift giving is a physical manifestation of this approach; it is an emotional, spiritual, and psychological act just as much as a concrete one.

When I arrived for the first time in Little Buffalo for academic purposes, I brought with me a 'research design and project.' When I began my PhD work, I described my requirements in terms of a 'collaborative research design' for the bureaucratic purposes of the university and the Social Sciences and Humanities Research Council team within which I was funded. In the next section I explain how the Lubicon translated collaborative research into Lubicon research.

Collaborative? The Lubicon Way

I first visited Little Buffalo in the fall of 1989. I spent only a week there, but the relationship grew when the chief visited Six Nations the following month to discuss his issues with the traditional governing body of the Haudenosaunee. The following December I found myself on a plane with Elder/Chief/Faithkeeper Henry Joe. We were on our way to assist the Lubicon chief and council in a ceremony. From there we travelled a dozen times back and forth to answer their calls for spiritual help and moral support. I decided to continue my research with the Lubicon, which meant continuing my graduate education, which sponsored many of the trips. There is no question that the Lubicon inspired me to continue my graduate education. The agreement drawn up with the team that funded my research demanded an 'articulated partnership,' which was no problem. But the same team wanted a clearly articulated collaborative research design, and this posed difficulties. It was fruitless to continually hound Lubicon Chief Ominayak and his council to help me articulate our research project – its design goals, time frame, and so on. The frustration I experienced in my efforts to extract a written agreement from them versed on seismic. I was never given a serious answer – just silence and grins and a 'whatever' attitude.

In time I came to realize that the Lubicon were *showing* me what they thought important instead of articulating their views. Eventually they invited me to their sweat lodge ceremonies, seasonal Tea Dances, feasts, Round Dances, and quiet meetings with Elders, which were held in the bush beside Fish Lake. They often explained the significance of each event in one-to-one discussions or formal interviews. The Lubicon actively resisted conforming to the research 'mandate' of positioning me as a researcher; at times, this frustrated my academic requirements for funding. The silence of the Lubicon leadership when I pleaded for help in developing a research design confused me many times. In hindsight, it is clear that when they attended meetings with the research team in Montreal, they were simply performing a reciprocal act. They wanted me in the field, but not for the purposes the research team had in mind. My value in the community related to my identity as a Mohawk woman – a much more prestigious positioning than that of researcher.

In early fall of 1991, I attended two Tea Dances. Tea Dances are annual social and spiritual gatherings, and are held in the fall and winter. I understood the basic concept of the Tea Dance: it is an occasion during which all medicines are blessed and people feed their ancestors. The medicine man who hosts the Tea Dance hires cooks and invites relatives and friends to share in the all-night ceremony. The ceremony is important as a time for sharing information and providing help to those in need. The social and political exchanges among the leaders who attended the Tea Dances in Little Buffalo were crucial to generating moral support for the Lubicon land claim.

The leaders and Elders who attended Lubicon Tea Dances were often also present at court proceedings and other important political meetings. The Lubicon leaders often asked Confederacy leaders from Six Nations to attend court proceedings and to help them in ceremonial matters. They also asked for meetings between the two nations. The Lubicon not only hosted the ceremonies but also travelled often to other areas to attend ceremonies: Sun Dances in Saskatchewan; feasts with Mohawk who had been involved in Oka; Round Dances in Hobbema; and Longhouse socials at Six Nations. During these ceremonies, quiet deliberations often took place among spiritual leaders, Elders, and political leaders. That political information as well as spiritual and moral support were being exchanged was affirmed through the traditional exchanges: the Lubicon received support and in turn pledged to support their like-minded 'friends.' For example, they quietly maintained a 'sacred fire' for the Mohawk during the stand-off at Oka. In return, the Mohawk and Six Nations traditional leadership attended several court appearances for Lubicon who were on trial. My arrival at Little Buffalo no doubt had an impact on the traditional-based reciprocity system and helped strengthen the collective struggle for the land.

As I have mentioned, when I first came to Little Buffalo, the Lubicon seemed to resist helping me articulate a collaborative research project. Their approach was very subtle – and if you know anything about the People of the Flint, the Mohawk, you know that subtlety is not our strength. For more than two years I could not be sure of what they wanted of me, and academically, I was becoming very insecure about my research focus. Not until 1991 did I realize that their agenda had been crystal clear all along. The Lubicon way of communicating had a more profound impact on my project than any written agreement would have. They felt that the Western approach was a false construction of our relationship, so they were delineating my role in Indigenous terms. They were willing to tolerate my research, but they also believed strongly that our relationship was much more than an academic partnership and that my academic research in the community was secondary to them.

An Indigenous researcher is both an insider and an outsider. You're an insider in terms of your identity as an Indigenous person, but your purpose there – the research – places you as an outsider. According to Linda Smith, (1999, 13–14), 'one of the many criticisms that gets levelled at Indigenous intellectuals or activists is that our Western education precludes us from writing or speaking from a "real" and authentic indigenous position ... It positions indigenous intellectuals in some difficult spaces both in terms of our relations with indigenous communities and within the Western academy.'

The academic experience itself is often colonizing, and this often works against projects that set out to support Indigenous autonomy and communities. Indigenous anthropologists are unique in that, having been rooted in the experience of colonialism, they are then denied the right to present that experience as they understand it.

At a meeting in the bush near Fish Lake, the Elders and others discussed everything from land claim offers, to the impact those offers would have on their communities and grandchildren, to their vision for the political, social, and spiritual direction of the community. The Elders – specifically Felix Laboucon – emphasized to the younger men present how important it was to save and promote cultural and spiritual ways if the Lubicon hoped to survive. Laboucon reminded everyone present how animals and people were suffering from the exploitation of the land. This sounded so familiar – was it Margaret Mead or Frantz Fanon?

According to a friend, this same group of Elders had decided several years earlier to focus on saving the culture by bringing back the old ways of doing things, but in a modern setting. In the 1950s some Elders had stopped performing ceremonies because the missionaries disapproved. As a result, some Elders were unwilling to openly discuss spiritual and ceremonial matters.

To rejuvenate their community, the Lubicon would need to restructure their present-day system of band council governance and to bring back their political, spiritual, and philosophical traditions. To this end, they instituted an Elders Council and decided to hold more of its meetings away from the band office, out on the land.

The agenda of the Lubicon became clearer to me. Through a process I refer to as 'sorting out the sacred,' they would decide what was to remain collectively private and what could be presented for public consumption (including to anthropologists). Questions regarding what constitutes sacred knowledge are deeply personal, and Elders are key guides and advisers in the decision process. For example, the political body of the Lubicon had been directed by Elders to stop the process of colonization and outside domination. The Elders advised the political body to recruit suitable outsiders if necessary, and to revitalize ceremonies. The Lubicon had set out not only to save their traditional ways but also to restructure their community in a traditional, non-Western context. My Haudenosaunee membership and knowledge became an

Dwight Gladue and Summer Joe. Photograph by Tom Hill, Woodland Cultural Centre, 1992.

asset to the Lubicon in their project of reconstituting their traditional belief system. The building of the Longhouse became a symbol of resistance within Lubicon territory as much as a symbol of respect. It offered an alternative space for conducting business – a space that served better than the band council office, which was tainted by colonialism.

The task of an Indigenous researcher is to sort out experiences through writing about them. What belongs and what does not? Linda Smith (ibid., 36) elaborates: 'If we write without thinking critically about our writing, it can be dangerous. Writing can also be dangerous because we reinforce and maintain a style of discourse which is never innocent. Writing can be dangerous because we sometimes reveal ourselves in ways which get misappropriated and used against us.' Smith's words highlight some of the problems I encountered while writing this book.

The Lubicon take pride in the lack of power the government has over them. They are often excoriated by government officials as 'bad Indians.' The ceremonies sponsored by the political leaders help bind together the symbolic and cultural collective consciousness of everyone involved. After one such ceremony, ex-chief Walter Whitehead (1989, interview) told me: 'You see, this is what the government is really afraid of. They have no power here, no control, they don't own this – our minds and souls become so strong, we are reminded with each ceremony that honors all the creations, the animals, the trees, the water, all life, what we are really fighting for. The spirits, the grandfathers, let us know who is really in power.'

Children are often persuaded to participate in ceremonial gatherings. While I was at Little Buffalo, young drummers from Joseph Bighead Reserve in Saskatchewan were often brought into the community to drum and sing and to informally teach traditions to young Lubicon. The unstated goal was to counter the young people's emerging view that tradition is 'uncool.' These efforts to reinstitute community cultural pride and autonomy, and to reclaim and revitalize all things Cree, were acts of decolonization.

In Indigenous settings such as the bush or the Longhouse, lawyers, advisers, and government officials were the marginal people and the Lubicon were in charge. The importance of Elders was always made clear, and so were their responsibilities. Women spoke about the importance of learning about the land and common respect and about the unimportance of material things. Teaching the young people to cherish

Haudenosaunee and Lubicon men building the Longhouse, Little Buffalo, Alberta, 1992.

who they are was an uphill battle, given the pressures of Western culture.

Lubicon Women

The Lubicon women often asked me about the role of Clanmothers in Mohawk society. In the early summer of 1992, the chief asked me to help the women get together and involve themselves in legal and social proceedings. At that time, the women also expressed their desire to 'help the chief, the land claim, and each other' (Women's Circle Meeting, 1992). The Lubicon Lake Nation Women's Circle began to meet biweekly; its members also attended political meetings and helped with speaking engagements. They set out to develop a community-oriented social service program by sponsoring healing circles, teen dances, and many other community events; they also supported cultural survival by teaching crafts and bush skills. They hired me as their part-time coordinator to begin a project that would train several women to take over the coordination and facilitation of human services at Little Buffalo.

Writing about these women is a far easier process as they were not involved in sensitive political negotiations. I could speak with them freely and in like-minded ways that were unrestrained by the spiritual (that is, sacred ceremonial) and political matters that the men were dealing with. My children were always with me, and this sealed their positioning of me as an Indigenous woman who valued her family. They understood me as another struggling Indigenous woman and bonded easily with my family.

After five years with the Lubicon, I realized that they had maximized my presence in all areas: as a woman, a Mohawk, and a professional. I no longer felt the need to ask them what they wanted from my collaborative research project.

Interaction with the men was difficult in that women normally don't interfere in the men's business. We supported the men and worked as interdependent entities. At Little Buffalo, there is a common respect for the roles of each gender. In gathering information about the men, I followed the dynamics and protocol that they themselves had developed. In gathering information about the women, it was easy to identify with their experiences, and this led to a comfortable space, even when it came to the writing of this book. This gender dynamic has done much to shape my presentation of the Lubicon; most obviously, the chapters that follow are structured on the basis of gender. In a way, this chapter division reflects a segregated tradition, one that has been misunderstood by Eurocentric scholars, who assume that this sort of segregation amounts to the degradation of women. In fact, the separation of the Lubicon men and women in the following chapters reflects a long-existing duality in Lubicon culture: men and women are separate yet intimately connected.

An earlier draft of this work was given to the chief to review, and others passed it on to community members. Community feedback was minimal; most people wanted only to read their own interviews. Few changes were made – by women, men, or political representatives. The women wanted to use the work as a vehicle for telling their story to the world. It was understood that the Lubicon themselves would own the final product and that they would have the right to release or not release the work. Many researchers who claim partnership maintain sole ownership in the end. Indigenous researchers are all too familiar with the exploitation of Indigenous communities and must approach their work as a collective project, one that places the community's interests, well-being, and authority above all else. As Smith reminded us earlier, writing can be dangerous. The Lubicon knew from painful experience how governments manipulate information – an issue I will discuss later.

Fred Lennerson has long been gathering information about the Lubicon that has been invaluable to the band council. He has a basement full of letters, memos, and other records pertaining to Lubicon history. Thanks to this preliminary work, I was able to spend my time differently. Chief Bernard Ominayak (1991, interview) told me not to 'focus on gathering more stuff, papers. Being in the community is better.' He was right. As I sifted through boxes of documents, I came to realize that something critical was missing about the Lubicon: the Lubicon people. Their culture was missing, and so was their everyday reality, and even more dramatically, so were the roles of women and their children.

I spent as much time with the Lubicon people as I could. As contributors, the youth were as important as the adults and the Elders. Every Lubicon is perceived as having significant experiences and insights to share. Social realities are shaped by people's varied experiences of the world. In the circumstances, the intergenerational approach came naturally to my research. My children visited their children. They asked brilliant questions, and I in turn asked perhaps not so brilliant questions. Because my two daughters were with me in Little Buffalo, I quickly realized that young people have a lot to say, and some of the most profound information I gathered came from them. There is no doubt that the value of the Lubicon voice in this text is immeasurable. Only the Lubicon can articulate how the destruction of the land has affected their lives and culture.

My first interviews were with the Lubicon leaders. It took time and effort for me to gain the confidence of people less used to 'talking to outsiders,' but in the end they all made significant contributions to the research. The Elders played a significant role in the community-based research. Because I had initially brought an Elder from my community, the Lubicon Elders were the first to position me.

When you grow up in or around Indigenous people, you're always asked, 'Who's your mom and dad or gramma and grampa?' Tribal linkages are about families, not status or class. This is an Indigenous way of contextualizing people who are not familiar. When I visit another community, the questions are broadened to, 'Where are you from and where did you grow up?' Mohawk or not, the Lubicon people needed to understand who I was, why I was so far from home, and what I wanted from them. They questioned my upbringing, my family attachments, and my educational background. Once at ease with my answers, they shared information about themselves. They often asked for cultural knowledge about my people, and in exchange they shared their cultural knowledge with me. This reciprocal trust seemed to be the underlying dynamic of my relationship with the Lubicon, and it continues to this day. The Lubicon methodological process of interviewing – which involves kinship positioning and reciprocity – is prevalent in all the Indigenous communities I have ever visited.

A Note on the Woodland Cree

The Woodland Cree are a band of Cree that the federal government organized in the late 1980s. Most reside at Codotte Lake. Codotte Lake is 15 kilometres from Little Buffalo. The federal government attempted to set them up as a 'dissident Lubicon band,' though few Lubicon signed onto membership (Goddard 1992). No interviews were conducted with the Woodland Cree because I was identified as a 'Lubicon supporter.' There were tensions between the Woodland Cree and the Lubicon, and I had no interest in getting caught in the middle. During this historical moment, I was concentrating mostly on interviews with the Lubicon; the government was out in full force trying to sign Lubicon members to the Woodland Cree band list. The Woodland Cree became victims of government: they were offered money, housing, and jobs. The Woodland Cree are not the bad guys here, the government is. The views expressed by the Lubicon about the Woodland are harsh, so please remember that this was at the height of the government's campaign to wipe out the Lubicon. The stakes were high as were the emotions.

Time Frame

The actual time I spent in Little Buffalo from 1989 until 1994 was about ten months. The longest periods we (meaning me and my immediate family) spent in the community were the summers of 1991 and 1992. Since 1992 I have travelled to Little Buffalo twelve times for seven to fifteen days. For their part, the Lubicon have travelled to my community twelve times since 1989. I keep in touch by phone – biweekly or monthly – with the women, and I continue to take notes and receive information. There is no set time frame as far as my 'research' is concerned. My research can be understood as taking place on 'Indian time,' which is essentially timeless. In this sense, I have never been completely out of the field. I continue to interact with the Lubicon spiritually and physically, often enough that I always know who is sick, who is having a hard time, and what is happening politically and socially. I have often attended Tea Dances, and I have gone to Little Buffalo to reinterview people as recently as the summer of 2004. At times, distance has been a real barrier, especially in times of death or some other crisis. Many times, we have felt badly about not being able to support one another at funerals, simply because we cannot afford to attend.

My ongoing involvement cannot be interpreted as 'going Native.' The Lubicon do not look to me for solutions, nor do I look to them for an identity. I know who I am. The ongoing kinship framework – an Indigenous framework of accountability and responsibility – is a part of our lives. The idea of 'being in the field' distorts the reality of the Lubicon relationship. More than likely, I'll be involved with them on and off for as long as time permits. In a way, this work always seemed incomplete; it is a superficial time frame that has imposed a conclusion when, really, the story is far from over. What is captured here is no more than a moment in their lives. Huron scholar George Sioui illustrates in his *For An Amerindian Autohistory*:

> What method could we use to write about them [EuroAmericans] in a respectful manner, given that their written tradition is unreliable and that, besides, we do not know them and are unable to comprehend their feelings and values? The reply of autohistory is that we should let *them* talk, talk about themselves, and thus avoid developing weighty, risky theories. (Sioui 1992, 102)

Voices from the Others

For those not immersed in the disciplines of native studies, anthropology, or social science, or connected to a university at all, much of what I am discussing might prove to be quite useless. Why take the time to articulate the critical issues bound within social scientific inquiry? This is for the benefit of Indigenous students. Since my research in Lubicon, I have been teaching in the 'local' Indigenous Studies program at McMaster University (thirty minutes from the rez!). I know the agony felt by incoming students trying to articulate why they think and feel differently from those in academia. While our people try to organize their critique of Western approaches and theory, they are trying to articulate 'original thought' in first year! The privilege of belonging to the dominant culture becomes a pronounced reality in each classroom. Non-Native students are completely comfortable, as they should be, with what is presented in the ivory tower. I struggle with the inherent assumption in social science courses which assumes an 'inferiority' of 'undeveloped' peoples or an 'inability' for them to 'adapt.' The reality is that our students conduct original research and construct original thought in their first year, since most turn to Elders, the community, and parents for validation and criticism of Western assumptions. As a rule (for those not familiar with academia), one is not expected to construct original thought until graduate school. This illustrates the structural inequality in knowledge production. I explained this to Chief Bernard. I asked if I could address these issues for the empowerment of students in this book, and he said 'go ahead.'

The Anthropological Question – *For you, you know who you are*

Our greatest contributions to humanity are no great earthworks, pyramids and such. Our greatest contribution is to leave the land as we found it. (Coon-Come 1989)

The Western yardstick that is used to measure all 'others' is beginning to reveal its ethnocentricity. Development, industrialization, and technology – all once considered signs of the advancement of a civilized society – are beginning to be seen as destructive forces that endanger life in all its forms, not just Native life. Some scientists are turning to 'Indigenous' wisdom to raise the consciousness of Western people and their institutions in fields such as environmental studies, feminism, health, and conflict resolution. A theoretical crisis in anthropology – and in the social sciences generally – has developed around the issues of resistance, representation, authority, textuality, analysis, and post-colonialism.

In this section I outline the current debates surrounding representation and postmodernism, reviewing some of the literature by contemporary scholars. I will use both Indigenous and non-Native sources to develop a framework for this story. Perhaps we can make room for ourselves in the dominant discourse by just being ourselves, by using one another for reference points rather than for anthropological theoretical arguments. The deconstruction of Western anthropological notions is perhaps the least productive process one can engage in. Constructing Indigenous Knowledge for the purpose of making an intellectual contribution is a far more worthy and interesting project. An Elder once pointed out to me, 'Be positive. Don't use your energy to be negative and tear "them" down. If you do, then you are one of them. You're behaving like them.' If I ever adopt the same disrespectful, arrogant behaviour of our oppressors, the assimilation process will have been complete. Henry Joe reminded me of the respect the Haudenosaunee show for other people's beliefs and of their desire to share rather than control. Anthropology has long controlled the definitions, data, and representations of my people. What I want to achieve here is a dialogue of mutual respect. These are my reasons for not accepting anthropological discourse and for proposing to build an Indigenist one.

Having said that, anthropological practice cannot simply be ignored. As an Indigenous person trained in classical anthropology, I am proposing an understanding of anthropology's global attack. No one individual can articulate the history of imperialism, or of colonialism. Anthropologists' actions have damaged Indigenous cultures. Clearly, anthropologists must come to terms with their perennial lack of respect for Indigenous Knowledge. At this point, the best relationship they can build is one based on the sharing of authority.

For evidence of how powerful anthropology has become as a discipline, one need only watch how Indigenous Knowledge is ritually appropriated every year at the Canadian Anthropological Society conference. On one of these occasions, in 1993, I had just come from Lubicon territory and had committed myself to presenting my SSHRC-funded research. I arrived late and studied the program. Wow. Native everything – land claims, culture, religion, poverty, health ... you name it, it was on their program. I expected to see representatives listed for all the Indigenous peoples. Two days later, I heard that a few Native women were attending. I never found them. I found only non-Native professors milling around discussing our cultures, land claims, and so forth. Everyone there was an authority on Native people, but no one was Indigenous. I was overwhelmed. The one Indigenous anthropologist there surpassed my wildest imagination by being cold, harsh, and demeaning. After long discussions with my friend from home, she told me, 'It's the "exotic factor." She's been the peacock for so long, it's hard for her to move over for an up-and-coming Indigenous woman. You're a threat to the throne.'

Another anthropologist known as a Lubicon 'advocate' at the conference stopped me in the hallway and asked, 'What exactly do you think you are doing with the Lubicon?' I stammered, 'Uh, well, in what sense?' She snorted, 'Building a Longhouse? You're imposing your culture on these people and confusing them!' I replied, 'Well, you better tell the Elders right away that I'm doing that, and Bernard. I'm sure they need you to point that out to them.' At that point, my idealist notions – about scholars and the capacity of anthropologists to deal respectfully and intelligently with Native issues – went right out the window. The 'allies' I thought I had at the conference had just given me a swift kick. I do not go to CASCA conferences anymore, nor do I hold expectations for anyone other than myself. Since I cannot in good conscience engage in hostile relations with 'older people,' I have withdrawn myself from anthropology circles.

Voices from the Margins

The crisis of ethnology is bound up in the historical, social, and political climate of Western post-colonialism. The voice of the 'other' was not so much sought after; rather it was merely permitted into a discourse that cast, coded, objectified, and dichotomized 'others' in an inferior position. The goal of anthropology to grasp the 'Native point of view' is a contextualized goal. The classic, anthropologically objectified, dissected Native is used to promote one theory after another (Berkhofer 1978; Churchill 1992). Sioux scholar Vine Deloria articulates this point. He states:

> Underneath all the conflicting images of the Indian one fundamental truth emerges: the white man knows he is alien and he knows that North America is Indian – and he will never let go of the Indian image because he thinks that by some clever manipulation he can achieve an authenticity which can never be his. (Deloria, cited in Churchill 1992, 39)

Modern anthropologists are beginning to reflect on how their appropriation of and claims to ownership over Native culture is an exercise of colonial power. They are in turn acknowledging the authority of the 'other.' Minh-Ha Trinh's *Native, Women, Other: Writing Postcoloniality and Feminism* (1989) explains this critical juncture in anthropology:

> The ultimate goal of every ethnographer, the Great Master wrote, is to grasp the native's point of view ... to realize *his* vision of *his* world ... This line has become the famous formula of nativist belief, the anthropological creed par excellence. In other words skin, flesh and bone – or, if one prefers the Great Master's terms in a reverse order: skeleton, flesh-blood and spirit ... Keeping such cannibal anthropological rites in mind, one can only assent to the following remark by an African man: 'today ... the only possible ethnology is one which studies the anthropophagus behavior of the white man.'

As an Indigenous woman 'other' in anthropology, I know that even my voice is inherently obscured and consumed in the discourse of my 'otherness.' There is a contradiction between being Indigenous and being an anthropologist; one is at once the subject/object and an 'authority.' As a Mohawk woman, I have been socialized to defer to Elders as the authorities. The key for me is to avoid the hegemonies of both worlds, to illuminate their forces, and, most important, to redefine my role as an anthropologist. In my terms, it is possible for being an Indigenous anthropologist to make perfect sense. As Mohawks of the Haudenosaunee people, we refer to ourselves as Ongwehonwe, 'human being or real person' and we are taught to respect others and to use our minds in a good way.

The Anthropologist Problem from an Indigenous Knowledge Base

James Clifford and George Marcus (1986) address the crisis of representation. Clifford argues that, since Malinowski, the method of participant observation has been heavily biased towards 'objective distance' even while recognizing the subjective. Classical ethnographies separate the 'subjectivity of the author from the objective referent of the text' (Clifford and Marcus 1986, 13). By convention, authoritative ethnographies often enlisted historical allegories to construct representations that spoke to one another and not with 'their subjects.' Whether it was a question of origins, evolution, or primitive society, ethnographers often used others to cast their theories or to project the European 'primitive selves.'

Asad (1986) argues that functionalist anthropologists were long concerned with explaining rather than describing. The functionalist approach to primitive thought was misleading for several reasons. First of all, functional anthropologists through their evaluative measures polarized the civilized and the savage. In doing so, they transformed their subjects' coherence within the functionalist discourse, and this amounted to an exercise of power. Structural ethnocentrism is said to transform subjects into objects (ibid., 142–6).

In the 1960s the balance between the subjective and the objective was disturbed. Clifford's analysis of classic and recent ethnographies brings to light the difficulties inherent in the new dialogical modes. The shift from the authority of the author, who narrates over the voice of the 'other' in order to represent them 'correctly,' causes a 'polyvocal text' to emerge. Clifford argues that 'once dialogism and polyphony are recognized as modes of textual production, monophonic authority is questioned, revealed to be characteristic of a science that has claimed to respect cultures' (in Clifford and Marcus 1986, 15).

Clifford (1983) analysed past ethnographic analyses and concluded that monological authority reflects an 'ethnographic consciousness' monopolized by Western culture (ibid., 52). A better representation of the 'other' begins with a sharing of positions of authority and voice. Research should be inherently dialogical.

Paul Rabinow (in Clifford and Marcus 1986, 242) contends that Clifford is a parasite who is guilty of what he accuses other anthropologists of doing: 'The other for Clifford is the anthropological representation of the other. This means that Clifford is simultaneously more firmly in control of his project and more parasitical.'

Rabinow accuses Clifford of textually creating his own authority by feeding off the work of other ethnographers. He points out that ethnographic works are 'situational,' and he suggests that Clifford does not examine his own writings or even his own situation. This, however, does not invalidate Clifford's work. Rabinow argues that dialogism is a poor solution, because it still amounts to controlled contextualization. Beyond dialogic texts are heterglossic texts – those which accord with authorship to the collaborators (ibid., 246). He outlines the shift from Clifford's modernism to postmodernism, which involves the rejection of hierarchies, dry histories, and the use of images. He argues that post-modernism is (as also suggested by Jameson) culturally and historically beyond stylism. Postmodernism is a 'period marker': the beginning of a new era of thinking and writing. Jameson argues that the Third World and unconsciousness have now been eliminated from nature and that restructuring will soon take place on a massive scale. In other words, the notion of the primitive has no place in social analysis today; thus, speaking about speaking for the other is no longer useful. As Rabinow (ibid., 250) suggests of Jameson's analyses:

> Although Jameson is writing about historical consciousness, the same trend is present in ethnographic writing: interpretive anthropologists work with the problem of representations of others' representations, historians and metacritics of anthropology with the classification, canonization, and 'making available' of representations of representations of representations. The historical flattening found in the pastiche of nostalgia films reappears in the meta-ethnographic flattening that makes all the world's cultures practitioners of textuality.

In short, Rabinow is suggesting that Clifford's own dialogue is not about the 'other'; rather, it speaks 'to one another.' The problem within dialogism has little to do with two subjects engaging in discourse.

Rather, dialogism is not speaking at all about other cultures; it is simply meta-anthropology. The basic focus has still been shifted from the voice of the 'other' to 'our' voice. Perhaps anthropologists' behaviour has turned on itself. Clifford and Rabinow are devouring each other in an effort to understand each other.

Renato Rosaldo (1989) sheds some light on the crisis of representation by proclaiming a subjective humanity. True to postmodernism, he argues that experience over time is important to an ethnographer's ability to interpret alien cultures. Thus one can say that interpretations are provisional, situational, and historical. As Rosaldo (ibid., 21) puts it:

> The agenda for social analysis has shifted to include not only eternal verities and lawlike generalizations but also political processes, social changes, and human differences. Such terms as *objectivity, neutrality,* and *impartiality* refer to subject positions once endowed with great institutional authority, but they are arguably neither more or less valid than those of more engaged, yet equally perceptive, knowledgeable social actors. Social analysis must now grapple with the realization that its objects of analysis are also analyzing subjects who critically interrogate ethnographers – their writings, their ethics, and their politics.

The importance of the new ethnography lies in the realization that it is the 'others' who are now situating ethnographers. In effect, they are 'raising the consciousness of the unconscious.' Self-reflection cannot be entirely credited to those who are self-consciously self-reflecting, since it has also been stimulated by the 'other.'

Cleverly, Rosaldo turns literal ethnography on his own culture. His analysis of a family breakfast exemplifies how objectification falls short of enabling one culture to understand another. He asks, 'Why does the highly serious classic ethnographic idiom almost inevitably become parodic when used as self-description?' (ibid., 22). Objective ethnographic descriptions can both reveal and conceal aspects of social reality. Classical defamiliarized ethnographic descriptions are neither accurate nor true nor humane. The humanization of ethnography is perhaps the greatest dilemma in the study of other humans. Rosaldo suggests that some dialogical potentials entail critical reflection and reciprocal perceptions, but these rarely reach open anthropological discourse.

Rosaldo argues for a processual analysis that refrains from claiming a monopoly on truth. He emphasizes perspectives that are not necessarily able to achieve summation. Geertz and Turner played key roles in the development of processual analyses. Case studies and analyses of social drama have allowed other theorists to demonstrate how few accounts of power relations and social inequality can succeed (ibid., 94). The work of Kenneth Burke (1969) describes processual analysis as an 'ongoing conversation' that is already in progress and that will continue after one departs. As Rosaldo (ibid., 104–5) states:

> Recent social thinkers have updated Burke's style of analysis by identifying the interplay of 'structure' and 'agency' as a central issue in social theory. Most central for them, in other words, is the question of how received structures shape human conduct, and how, in turn, human conduct alters received structures ... Marx's dictum stresses the interplay of structure and agency, rather than granting primacy to one or the other ... to focus on the unfolding interplay of political struggles, social inequalities, and cultural differences.

Analyses of the interplay between structure and agency are insufficient in some areas. One of those areas relates to 'feelings' or humanness, both of which are often underanalysed. Raymond Williams's (in ibid., 106) structure of feelings imagines that society cannot be reduced to fixed norms: 'Structures of feeling differ from such concepts as "world-view" and "ideology" because they are just emerging, still implicit, and not yet fully articulate.' Understandings of human social interaction and the everyday have significantly influenced contemporary works of social theory (ibid., 108).

Questions remain: What does all of this say about the 'Native' voice? Does the 'other,' who is not yet allowed the privileged position of consciousness, get to 'feel' the oppression? And is it unconscious cognition that determines their behaviour? Have Natives as humans with feelings ever had the opportunity to express their social wisdom?

Postmodern theorists have acknowledged their own positions of power, subjectivity, and historicism in processes of social analysis. Perhaps it is time to turn the crisis in anthropology over to the 'other.' Dense descriptions of a postmodern and anti-imperialist sort continue to drown out the 'other's' voice. The notion of grasping the Native perspective has been obscured by self-reflection, self-justifications, and global interpretations of the self rather than the 'other.' There is little room for the 'other' to carve out a true presence within the theoretical debates over analysis that are currently underway.

The foremost problem has to do with the privileged position of the ethnographer in relation to the 'unconscious other.' Until those in positions of privilege make room for the voice, knowledge, and consciousness of the 'other,' the Native point of view will always be a construction of the ethnographer. As Edward Said (1989, 220) stated, the Native point of view is not 'ethnographic fact'; it is a 'sustained adverbial resistance to the discipline and ... political dominance ... The manifestation of colonialism is through the configurations of power. The political culture of colonial rulers operated within frames of conquest, exploitation and representation to break existing social patterns and reassemble them according to European standards.' The problem with Indigenous knowledge as it is constructed by the dominant anthropological discourse is that it threatens to lead to intellectual assimilation. Hegemony is subtle, and the diffusion of the Indigenous voice into processual analyses can assimilate the intellectual into a hegemonic ideology. If we allow our voices to simply serve the dominant agenda, to reaffirm one dominant theory over another, to submit to yet another form of appropriation, then exploitation and objectification will emerge in anthropological texts. To this, Taiaiake Alfred (1999, 132) adds:

> What is needed in countries like Canada and the United States is the kind of education that would force the general population to engage with realities other than their own, increasing their capacity to empathize with others – to see other points of view and to understand other people's motivations and desires ... However, indigenous people have succeeded in altering non-indigenous people's perceptions through dialogue in institutions of higher learning ... These leaders will practice a new style of Native politics that will reject the colonial assumptions and mentalities that have allowed state domination to continue. It will recognize and counter the state's efforts to co-opt, divide, and conquer communities.

An awareness of leadership and intellectual traditions will prevent Indigenous issues, debates, and ideas from bleeding into the Western vacuum of 'other' discourse. We must begin to 'talk to each other' in order to stop anthropology or any 'ology' from subverting the development of Indigenous Knowledge. If we engage in attempts to validate ourselves 'through anthropologists' eyes,' we will only slide back into colonization. My interest is in decolonization – in rebuilding our knowledge.

Trinh Minh-ha (1989, 80) reveals how the segregation of the 'other' inevitably signals that *they* (the other) are a deviation from *us* (the Euro-American):

> Such an attitude is a step forward; at least the danger of speaking for the other has emerged into consciousness. But it is a very small step indeed, since it serves as an excuse for their complacent ignorance and their reluctance to involve themselves in the issue. You who understand the dehumanization of forced removal-relocation-reeducation-redefinition, the humiliation of having to falsify your own reality, your voice – you know. And often you cannot *say* it.

Not Seeking Approval – But Respect

Though we as Indigenous people live and breathe our ways, we have yet to come up from underground to really 'say it like it is,' both for fear of reprisal and in order to protect the sacred. Those who dominate, rule in part through fear – that is, by instilling fear in the oppressed. Perhaps there is a certain amount of security and protection (self-preservation) in hiding one's feelings and thoughts from the oppressors – at least, until we realize that silence is the oppressors' goal. Silence is beyond 'false consciousness'; it is what we have had to resort to in order to survive over the past century. But we can no longer afford to remain silent. At the same time, if we enter into the 'scientific' arena of causes and effects, our knowledge will be denied access or validation in the broader context. For example, the Lubicon know that the destruction of the land and its animals is directly related to their poor health. If as a 'scientist' I were to state that this destruction has been directly responsible for the social problems of the Lubicon, I would be expected to measure the impact of that development. Yet, just as in the Grassy Narrows case, one cannot isolate variables to show a direct correlation between causes and effects on human beings. This suggests how governments and corporations are able to leave the 'burden of proof' on the backs of the oppressed. Laws have historically served the dominant; so too have the principles of some social science research, and in much the same way. But if the oppressed can succeed in changing the context from Euro-North American to Indigenous, and in recognizing the validity of their own 'natural-spiritual law,' then Indigenous Knowledge and oral testimony will be formally recognized and legitimated.

A Native 'science' contextualizes the spoken word as fact and places the collective experience of the group as a social truth. Linda Smith explains this process:

> The arguments of different indigenous peoples based on spiritual relationships to the universe, to the landscape and to stones, rocks, insects and other things, seen and unseen, have been difficult arguments for western systems of knowledge to deal with or accept. These arguments give a partial indication of the different world views and alternative ways of coming to know, and of being, which still endure within the indigenous world. Concepts of spirituality which Christianity attempted to destroy, then to appropriate, and then to claim, are critical sites of resistance for indigenous peoples. The values, attitudes, concepts and language embedded in the beliefs about spirituality represent, in many cases, the clearest contrast and mark of difference between indigenous peoples and the West. It is one of the few parts of ourselves which the West cannot decipher, cannot understand and cannot control ... yet.

In attempting to save ourselves, we face the dilemma of co-optation, of losing the sacred and exposing ourselves too readily to our oppressors. By moving our private knowledge into the public arena for consumption, deconstruction, and other shortcomings, we might only be playing a role in our own oppression. Yet when we move with great caution into European discourses, neither seeking approval nor trying to prove ourselves, we will be moving in the pursuit of social justice. As Robbie Robertson sang in 'Words of Fire, Deeds of Blood' (2006):

> Perhaps you think the Creator
> sent you here to dispose of us as
> you see fit
> If I thought you were sent by the
> Creator
> I might be induced to think you
> had a right to dispose of me
> But understand me fully with
> reference to my affection for the
> land
> I never said the land was mine to
> do with as I choose
> The one who has a right to
> dispose of it is the one who has

created it
I claim a right to live on
my land
And accord you the privilege to
return to yours

The late Seneca scholar John Mohawk (in Barreiro 1992, 24–5) addresses the issue of historical intellectualism in Indigenous societies through a comparative discourse about European 'enlightenment' and Haudenosaunee philosophy:

> It is said that the Conquistadors spilled more blood than any other group of people ever spilled up to that time, and that would be quite a contest if you know the history before that time. That mentality also said that they had to dehumanize the victims of the conquest. Two things were born of that. One was racism. Even modern scholars identify the period of conquest as the birth of racism in the modern world. It was the first time that arguments were seriously put forward in the courts of Spain, especially at Valladolid, arguing that the Indians were biologically inferior human beings, that they were not even human beings at all that they were really beasts of burden, that they were subhumans and therefore subject to the treatment of subhumans ... This denial of thinking among peoples other than Europeans was so great that when these two worlds came together, the people who wrote the history wrote the Indian thinking right out of the history because by the theories of the conquistador, the Indian could not think, a burro cannot think.
>
> So the very idea that Indians could have helped thinking among Europeans has been negated. There are still people who will swear to you that there were never any Indians who ever did any thinking that contributed in any concrete way to any of the institutions of the West.

Only recently have Western scholars examined the First Americans as interdependent societies with political, social, and economic structures that operate according to intellectually coherent principles.

Indigenous Discourse

The Indigenous societies of North America have a fundamental awareness of their relationship to the universe. This knowledge is undoubtedly spiritually based. It includes a bedrock understanding that human beings are not endowed with the right to dominate others or to destroy that which is around them. The animistic belief that every life form has a spirit and should be respected fuels discontent with any ideology that is based on domination.

Indigenous views take into account the humanization/subjectification of not only people but also animals, plant life, rocks, and all of Creation. This is not 'mythology' or even religion; it is a way of life, a reflection of the Native consciousness. This 'awareness' is complex in that it not only accounts for this world but also provides for guidance in the spirit world. 'Knowing' involves a developed sense of spiritual knowledge that informs behaviour and influences social actions. Dreams, visions, and prophecies can direct and inform Indigenous people in their everyday consciousness. More than that, 'knowing' empowers the Indigenous consciousness.

As mentioned earlier, Indigenous conceptualizations of power differ from those of the West, as do Indigenous notions of powerlessness. The possession of sacred knowledge confers power and demands respect. To be ignorant is to be powerless. As Feit (in Morrison and Wilson 1986, 182) explains of Cree power:

> The quest for power is a metaphor the Cree might use for the life as a hunter ... The concepts of the wind persons mediate and link several series of ideas that serve to order Cree world in space and time ... 'Power' is a relationship in thought and action among many beings, whereby potentiality becomes actuality. Hunting is an occasion of power in this sense, and the expression of this is that animals are gifts, with many givers ... The Cree have a distinct system of rights and responsibilities concerning land, resources, community, and social relations – a system of land and resource tenure, and of self-governance ... The land and animals are God's creation, and, to the extent that humans use or control them, they do so as part of a broad social community united by reciprocal obligations.

Accordingly, it is inaccurate to define power in terms of material possessions. In Indigenous arenas, to be powerless is to be unaware of who you are. To be weak is to display disrespect and ignorance.

The past, present, and future inform everyday actions in the political, social, economic, and spiritual spheres, which together constitute a whole. The Ojibway scholar James Dumont (1976, 32) has written:

> It is important to understand that it is not confined to a certain group, but

is a comprehensive, total viewing of the world and is essential for a harmony and balance amongst all of creation. This is, then, a *primary* kind of vision ... What is essential is not an impossible cross-the-culture leap of understanding but rather a return to a primal way of *seeing* ... A Midé Shaman from Minnesota expressed this same thought in this way: In the beginning, while the races still lived together as one, each of the races had to come to a decision as to what direction he would choose. During this time White Man and Red Man found themselves walking together along the same road. At some point in their journey they came to a division in their path. One of the two possible roads before them offered knowledge and growth through accumulation and mounting of all that could be seen ahead (a one-hundred-and-eighty-degree vision). This is what White Man chose and he has developed in this 'linear' and accumulative fashion ever since. The other road appeared less attractive materially and quantitatively, but offered a whole and comprehensive vision that entailed not only vision before but also vision behind (a three-hundred-and-sixty-degree-vision). This was a circular vision that sought to perceive and understand the whole nature of an object or event – its physical reality as well as its soul. The Red Man chose this road and he has developed in this circular and holistic way ever since... In modern times, especially, it is the one who chose the straight-ahead vision who must recognize the ultimate value in the all-around-vision, and, must see the necessity of returning to this more primal and total way of 'seeing the world.'

The value of a comprehensive approach is nested in a knowledge base that roots one in a strong and empowering foundation. Indigenist discourse is framed in a much different way from Western legal-economic discourse. It is true that the central issue is land and the control of resources that would allow Indigenous societies a degree of self-governance and self-determination. But the political dynamics involved in this are often informed by traditional beliefs. The assumption, even in the Lubicon case, is that Indigenous rights are conferred by the Creator. The resistance to colonial forces is, again, not a reaction to material colonial domination, but an expression of sacred knowledge given to the people by the Creator. Indigenous power through ceremonies has had to confront repeated efforts by colonists to wipe out such practices. Yet Indigenous Knowledge remains intact because of the oral mode of transmission. Indeed, Indigenous peoples have long participated in an ongoing dialogue. The experiential nature of Indigenous Knowledge has fostered a rich and total understanding. Individuals are recognized as 'wise and experienced' and are respected by their community as 'keepers of the culture.' Once one enters the Indigenous mode of learning, one finds that it is holistic and cumulative, not deconstructive. The subjective, human nature of inquiry is defined by several truths that an individual must be prepared to accept. Dumont elaborates on the significance of placing historical events within Indigenous historical constructions.

The dynamics of 'ordinary' and 'non-ordinary' realities within the Indigenous experience enable a deeper appreciation for Indigenous consciousness. We must go beyond ideology, beyond grounding events in ordinary and non-ordinary realities, in order to truly represent Native history. For example, the Lubicon are constantly drawing from ordinary and non-ordinary realities that directly and indirectly influence social events.

Visions, dreams, and spirit messages may result in an actual event taking place. I offer a specific example to demonstrate this further. In December 1992 a shaking tent ceremony was conducted by the Lubicon at Fish Lake, Alberta. A member of the community specifically requested the ceremony, to which I was invited. The questions the Lubicon asked the spirits related to the community's future direction. The spirits told them what to do spiritually, socially, politically, and individually. The spirits also stated that nothing should be repeated outside of the ceremony (which is why I cannot give any more details of what occurred during it). The advice given in the shaking tent resulted in concrete actions. It also went against some people's feelings; in other words, they could not do what they felt like doing. They had to set personal feelings aside in order to achieve a common good for all Lubicon.

In summary, if we are to fully understand the Lubicon, or any Indigenous society, we must fully consider the interconnections among those coexisting realities which fuel the social dynamics and ideological underpinnings of that society. Indigenous peoples assume that it is just as real to engage in a dialogue with the spirit world as it is with the physical. They assume that it is normal to believe that all of Creation has a spirit and that only the Creator can provide the laws we abide by. If we can consider an Indigenous understanding of knowledge, we can begin to fully comprehend Indigenous reality and issues, such as Native history, culture, resistance, spirituality, and so forth. We must place our 'facts' within an Indigenous context in order to represent the events more truthfully.

2 Voices from the Lubicon

Knowing Who We Are

The young men stood in a small circle holding their hand drums and began to sing. The older men rose, reaching out to hold hands with one another, and began to dance clockwise, lifting their feet rhythmically to the sound of the drum. The women and children joined the circle as an unbroken chain moved into the morning. The Elders we had assembled for the Roundhouse and gathering were from many nations, including the Cree, the Iroquois, and the Tlinkit. All had travelled long distances to Little Buffalo, an isolated community in northern Alberta, to pray for the Lubicon people. It had been decided early in the summer of 1992 by the medicine man from Little Buffalo that the 'good people' should come together because the 'bad people' had already joined forces. In broken English he told me of his dream about the good people needing to unite. Charlie, in his mid-forties, was tall with long braids and penetrating eyes. He seldom spoke, but when he did, you listened. Shortly after our conversation, the chief had asked me to organize this gathering. There was a shortage of 'material resources' but always an abundance of faith. It just so happened that the research team led by Colin Scott, which was funding my graduate work, had decided they should meet in the communities rather than at McGill University. As usual, it was my job to figure out a way to meet the Indigenous agenda by utilizing an academic agenda and resources! A few phone calls and a lot of praying seemed to work. The anthropologist research team should meet in Little Buffalo. The creative work of appeasing two worlds began again.

Organizing a gathering in Little Buffalo was a challenging experi-

Lubicon Elder Summer Joe, Fish Lake. Photograph by Tom Hill, Woodland Cultural Centre, 1992.

ence but also a collective one. The spiritual matters were taken care of by Charlie, the chief, John C. Leternder, and Henry Joe from Six Nations. Minor details, like financing Elders' transportation, and deciding whom to invite and how to accommodate everyone, were left to me. The women had just begun to organize as a group. They were excited about the visitors. Each family would take a turn cooking the meals for the three-day gathering. What they were going to cook, I did not know. Rosanne sent Dwight out to hunt for moose. Louisa Ominayak had her sons hunting for ducks, and her daughters went picking berries for the bannock and dessert. Maggie Auger sorted out the labour matters, such as who would clean, and found women to help out and billet the guests.

The next task was to figure out where to find the money for travel and food. I turned to the 'informal men's group.' These men had been strong supporters and friends of the Lubicon for many years. They attended the political meetings and spiritual gatherings in Little Buffalo. They were a small group but a strong one. Denys Auger, then vice president of the Alberta Indian Association, offered to find some funding. Chief Ernest Sundown, of the Joseph Bighead Reserve in Saskatchewan, also said he would help. Chief Victor Buffalo, from Hobbema, flew in to Little Buffalo to discuss the gathering and pledge his support. A traditional Seneca chief of the Iroquois Confederacy promised he would be there and bring a few others. The 'core group' was now in action; we just needed a date and to send out invitations.

The research team that supports my work had wanted to hold a meeting in Little Buffalo. I thought perhaps they could bring Elders and leaders with them. A few phone calls were made, and it all worked out. Colin Scott arranged to bring four anthropologists and Innu research partners Peter Peneshue, Daniel Ashini, and Johnny Grant from James Bay. We sent the word out on 21 August. The Elders from the blockade at Meadow Lake, Saskatchewan, would attend, as well as a traditional chief from the Tlinkit people in Alaska.

As August approached, several agendas emerged. The spiritual meaning of the gathering was the central focus, but it was never discussed openly. The women focused on social possibilities, organizing the feast, the Round Dance, softball games with Joseph Bighead, and the official opening of the newly built Longhouse. My research team's involvement required that a more formal 'meeting of minds' take place. The chief decided to invite the Lubicon lawyers to meet with the academics and decide what might be done to assist the Lubicon in a technocratic way. He also decided to have a formal discussion with Elders to ask for their advice.

Charlie, Henry Joe, and the chief had their agenda. Charlie had not been the only one to have a message given to him through dreams. Before leaving for Little Buffalo in June, he had also been contacted through dreams, and now he came over to discuss them. He wanted to tell Bernard that a sacred fire burned on Lubicon land and that a ceremony was to be conducted by our people in Little Buffalo. Henry Joe had two agendas: to help the Lubicon in their struggle, and to kill the self-government referendum of 1992, which he believed would be the 'demise of all Indians.' The sacred fire would 'burn that paper, see that it go up in smoke' (Henry Joe 1992). He believed that the Lubicon were involved in a spiritual war and that they needed to enlist the help of their ancestors, because only with that help could they get rid of the 'dark cloud over them' (Henry Joe 1992).

We met at the West Harvest Hotel in Edmonton on the evening of 16 June, 1992. In our cramped room, we offered tobacco to a guest who was visiting the area and who was known as a medicine man. This man, John, was asked to share his vision with the Lubicon. After lengthy discussions about various dreams and visions, the 'group' decided to have a sacred fire at Little Buffalo. The discussions were so serious and intense that we lost track of the time and our children! Bernard Ominayak's son, Lou, my girl, Ashley, and another friend's daughter were wreaking havoc in the hallways. This ended abruptly when a woman screamed, 'Where's your parents? Do you know what time it is?' We all sat very still, waiting to see if the kids would tell on us. I laughed as I observed the nervous looks in our room; all the 'radicals' held their breath as they waited to be scolded by the angry woman. Finally she slammed her door and the children quietly returned to our room. We all sighed with relief that they had not led her to our room. The meeting ended. The agenda for the summer's meeting had been set.

This gathering turned out to be central to that summer's visit to Lubicon. As we set up the tipi in Bernard's yard between the Longhouse and the sweat lodge, we sensed that events were coming together. The lawyers and academics had arrived with Peter Peneshue, Daniel Ashini, and Chief Able Bosum from the James Bay Cree. Lubicon lawyers James O'Reilly, Owen Young, Bob Sachs, and Ken Stroszik had arrived, as well as a number of anthropologists, including Colin Scott, Adrian Tanner, and the late Joan Ryan. The agenda for the day's meeting at the Longhouse had been set: it was to strategize for the upcoming trial of the Lubicon in the fall. The Lubicon faced criminal charges for allegedly burning down a logging camp. Those at the gathering viewed this act as political, not criminal, since it was associated with the land claim. After many hours of discussion, it was decided that the academics would gather 'cultural' information from Lubicon Elders in order to substantiate their history and dependence on the land. Joan Ryan was to bring in testimony from the Lubicon women regarding their experiences, and Ken Stroszik told me that I 'could work with the kids to see if they might contribute to testifying.' The Innu leaders offered their support to the Lubicon, and Chief Bosum cemented his support to their struggle. Then the lawyers left, and the Elders began to arrive.

I scurried around trying to find the people who had told me they would billet and help prepare the Longhouse for the meal. We held a Round Dance and feast that evening. The fire would be lit the following day, when all the Elders arrived. The van from Six Nations arrived with Chief Henry Joe and Elder Calvin Miller. Mohawk Chief Allan McNaughton was flying in later that day. All of these people had been to Little Buffalo for ceremonies earlier in the spring. Chief Victor Buffalo had sent five strong elderly women to participate in the events. The key people had arrived; the fire was to be lit by afternoon.

Men busied themselves getting wood and rocks for the four sweat lodge ceremonies that would take place over the next two days. People sat around the yard waiting for Bernard to begin the ceremonies. Elders entered the tipi, where Henry Joe burned tobacco for the fire. The pipe ceremony also began. Charlie prayed in Cree, and Henry Joe prayed in Cayuga. Charlie had advised Bernard to stay in the sweat lodge throughout the four consecutive sweats. We jokingly asked Charlie if Bernard was to be sacrificed for the ceremonies.

The first sweat began. Many people sat around the fire, which had been built outside the lodge, talking and joking. I busied myself finding keys to empty houses for the guests, tracking down the drummers from Joseph Bighead, and playing softball with the younger Lubicon. The women arrived at the Longhouse with the prepared food, and we cleaned as the guests began to arrive. The Round Dance was about to begin when I was asked to accompany the Elder into the sweat. Although the Elder had been to Little Buffalo on many occasions, he had never entered the sweat lodge. We were all happy that he finally had agreed to go in. I was supposed to orchestrate the Round Dance and help the shy Lubicon women greet the 'outsiders.' I also had to find beds for the many Elders from the Meadowlake blockade. I turned to Ernest and asked him if he would take over my duties.

People prayed out loud in their own language. Everyone was praying for Bernard to have the strength and wisdom to help his people as well as praying for the people and the land. Charlie sang four songs, as did Denys and Henry Joe. It was a strong sweat. We also prayed for the Elder to get well. In between rounds, the flap would open and Erwin, Bernard's eldest son, would pop his head in. After the first round he said, 'The Elders from Saskatchewan don't want to camp, they want a mattress.' After the next round, he said, 'Do you know what happened to the truck with the mattress for the Elders?' After the third round, he said, 'Do you know where the key to the house where we want to put the mattress is?' After the fourth, he popped his head in to ask, 'Do you know what happened to the Elders that wanted the mattress?' We burst into laughter and continued with the ceremonies.

When we left the lodge, the Northern Lights had arrived and surrounded us. I went into the Longhouse and was told to 'get Ernest away from the microphone. He's been telling bad jokes all night.'

The Longhouse was full to capacity, and everyone was dancing and enjoying themselves. Sitting outside trying to remember all that I had seen and heard that night, I wondered how I was going to write about my involvement in these ceremonies and closed political meetings. My role as researcher had been transformed by the Lubicon. They had shared so much with me; they had included me in their lives. They had revealed so much to me that was sacred and profound. How could this relationship be translated into the white man's world? As I listened to the drums, I felt lost between Canadian, Mohawk, and Cree worlds. How did a Mohawk woman end up with the Lubicon Cree in northern Alberta working on a doctorate in anthropology for McMaster University? It was all part of the Creator's mystery in life. I reflected on a conversation I had in 1990 with my supervisor, Harvey Feit. He had cautioned me that the Lubicon might not exist by the time I finished my research. I remembered walking away stunned from his office. Would I be able to deal with it?

Then I remembered I was here for a reason. I had been allowed to be a part of these ceremonies, which are a focal point of Lubicon life. I resolved to myself that people needed to know about the power of the grandfathers, the grandmothers, the fire, the drums and songs, the pipe, the Elders, the ceremonies and sweat lodge. They needed to know about the spirit of these original human beings – the Lubicon people.

The Longhouse, Little Buffalo, 1992. Photograph by Tom Hill, Woodland Cultural Centre.

Henry Joe sat with me for a while. I told him about my dilemma, and he replied, 'Write the truth, that's all.' So simple was his answer that, I had to laugh at myself. I told him that they wouldn't accept that there is a truth and that I might not even recognize it. He told me, 'Write from your mind and heart. What you heard from these people, what you saw, even what you felt, isn't that your responsibility, to tell their story?'

Henry Joe, a traditional chief and Faithkeeper, had been my companion on this journey from the beginning. In 1989 he had visited the community with me and my husband. By August 1992 we had visited the community many times together. The Longhouse they had built had inspired him. The building was finished in the summer of 1992, and the opening ceremony was conducted during the gathering. He had tried to help the people spiritually and morally over the past four years and this had earned their respect. I felt privileged to have been allowed to be a part of it all. In memory of this Elder, I will attempt to follow his advice.

Voices from the Lubicon

During our visits, my family and I spent most of our time with the Chief of the Lubicon Lake Nation, Bernard Ominayak. We usually stayed in his home. Quite soon, we felt like an extended family. I say 'extended' because so many of my relatives who accompanied me on my research trips – aunts, mothers, and nephews – referred to Bernard as 'uncle.' We spent a lot of time together; even so, it was difficult to find times when Bernard could discuss his life.

During the summer of 1991, I logged one ten-day period in Bernard's life. In ten days he drove to Edmonton and back three times, attended four meetings, and held at least seven sweat lodge ceremonies. He never went to bed before four a.m. To say the least, we could not physically or emotionally keep up with his gruelling schedule. His days and nights included meeting with Lubicon lawyers, attending a conference hosted by the Lutheran Church, fixing a furnace in a lady's home at two a.m., gathering rocks near Fish Lake for the sweat, and picking and making medicine for a sick little girl. One of the medicines he showed me consisted of eighty-four different herbs. This was one example of his many dozens of prepared medicines. He often stayed up while others went to bed, usually to prepare medicines for the community's many ill people. It was not unusual for him to spend the greater part of the night in the sweat lodge. He would eat at three a.m., visit a while, sleep, wake at nine a.m. to head to Edmonton for a one p.m. meeting, then return to Little Buffalo for another sweat by nine p.m. Throughout all this, he was still a hunter at heart, with a deep sense of obligation to his family and to many others. Besides carrying out his 'official' business, he was always on the scene when homes caught fire, when accidents happened, when there was a break-and-enter at the band store, when there were incidents of domestic violence, and so forth.

Living at his house was a lot like living at a twenty-four hour crisis centre. He was the community's hunter, doctor, policeman, fireman, social worker, and spiritual adviser; he was the Lubicon Chief. On top of the day-to-day official and unofficial business, there were always local reporters wandering around, as well as journalists from Japan, Germany, and Sweden. At times it was downright comical watching Bernard operate on five different levels simultaneously. Following is an account of events that took place at Fish Lake. All of our actions were under police surveillance – the logging camp that had been torched was quite near Fish Lake. The police sat parked outside Bernard's home, beside the cemetery across the road.

The Sacred Run, led by the former leader of the American Indian Movement, Dennis Banks, arrived that day. There were more than fifty

Lubicon Chief Bernard Ominayak, Chief Ernest Sundown, and Lubicon Elder
Edward Laboucon greeting the Sacred Runners, 1991.

runners, some Natives, the rest from the four corners of the world –
Africa, Europe, India, Sweden, and so on. We had a hot dog roast at
Edward Laboucon's to welcome the weary runners. We were planning
a feast for that evening. The food was trucked to Fish Lake, along with
the runners, who were short on vehicles.

Bernard had been extremely busy over the previous days and was
quite exhausted. The runners were anxious to talk with him about the
land claim, and he tried to hide in his cabin. Under normal circumstances, people do not bother him when he is in his cabin. They often
wait outside, weather permitting. Since these visitors were not accus-
tomed to Lubicon social mores, they walked into his cabin and surrounded him. At least twenty people crammed themselves in, sitting
everywhere. A woman from France was trying to show him an article
she had about the Lubicon. A Lakota man was talking medicine to him
while an East Indian man started to massage his back. Bernard looked
over his shoulder and said, 'That's okay. I don't need that.' The man
replied, 'Oh, yes, you are so tense. Let me rub you down.' He went
down Bernard's back and started to massage his legs. If I had a picture

of his face during that moment, it might show much of Bernard's character. He tried to pull back from the woman who was insisting he read the article, thrusting it so close to his face that his cap fell off. He came as close to losing his cool as I had ever seen. He pulled away from the East Indian man who had a hold of his legs, backed away from the woman, almost tripped over the people sitting on the floor, and headed straight to the door, only to be greeted by an RCMP officer. Those of us watching this episode were laughing quietly as he manoeuvred through this comical situation, which he was not appreciating one bit. The scene stuck with me. It captured so much of his life: the pressure from people demanding his attention, and the calm he summoned amidst total chaos.

The sweat lodge seemed to be the centre of his life, and over the years I watched him draw more and more of his strength from it. There was no chaos in the sweat lodge, and there were no white people. Everything in it was in Cree and in the control of the grandfathers.

The following interviews with him were conducted during the summers of 1991 and 1992 and warrant full transcription.

Chief Bernard Ominayak: 'This is a bloody war you know.'

'I was really close to my grandmothers. I remember when we were in the bush this one time. I must have been eight or nine. I knew someone was there, I knew she had passed away. My parents didn't know what to think. I wanted to keep going to see her. I guess it was then that I realized something about myself. I paid attention to those things after that. In the bush, you're closest to all those ways of knowing, close to God. I was sent to Grouard, the mission school. I didn't much like it but did like learning. I read the bible, I know what's in there, too. In fact, they used to have contests for kids who could memorize different testaments. I won. I really memorized the whole bible that year. I won a scrapbook. Some of the stories were interesting, but I liked the stories we were told better. Closer to those. I ran away after grade ten. I couldn't stand to be away for so long. I had a family soon after that I needed to look after. We lived in the bush and I would work when I could. No roads. I got involved in these land claims. The Elders told us about them and Walter was trying his best to figure out why we hadn't gotten a reserve and how we could deal with this issue. I would go with him to some meetings. I met people like Harold Cardinal, who also went to Grouard.

'The Isolated Communities Board was an initiative by [non-treaty signers] supported by Harold to deal with people like us, in our situation. I guess things just progressed from there. I read everything I could get my hands on and found myself as chief. It all seemed like a natural progression of events. Anyhow, Fred Lennerson was brought in by Harold and I liked the way he seemed to have all the facts with him. He was always prepared. The Isolated Communities Board started to fall apart, people not attending meetings, internal politics. But from our standpoint it was the only solid structure thus far to deal with our situation; I didn't want to see it fall apart. It did anyway. We didn't have a band council or anything at that point. Walter had managed to start at least getting housing. I bugged Fred, calling and calling him to come out here and help the Lubicon. I would call him from this pay phone at the only gas station in the area. I knew that if I kept it up he would give in. He did. Trapping skills can be used in many ways [laughs]. I knew Fred knew the government and I knew we did not. We needed Fred to show us the ropes, how these people operate, how they think. Fred wanted me to do all the talking and tell me later about it, but I wanted to just watch, watch white people, learn from observing them. So in most cases, I would sit back and listen, see where their priorities were. It was quite a lesson from what I was used to in the way I grew up. But Fred was fire, and I figured out you have to fight fire with fire, someone who knows their language. We would work together in that way.

'From there Fred worked with the Alberta Indian Association and we eventually lobbied for official recognition as a band council. Even that was a big struggle. I knew we needed a lawyer, given what was happening with the oil coming in, the roads. We needed legal advice. I asked Fred to get us the best. Fred [through Billy Diamond] managed to convince James O'Reilly to come out and hear our case. It wasn't easy, mind you, convincing people like this to work for you when you have nothing but a story to tell them. That was it, we were just up front with these guys. We knew what we wanted for a long time; it was just finding the white people to work with us in fighting the government. Actually, when you think about it, we must have been crazy to think we could do what we did, convincing these strangers to come here, with no money to offer. But the Elders were pushing us younger guys to settle this once and for all. I set my mind to it back then. I had babies to care for, mouths to feed, but I focused all my energies on getting this done, this land claim. When I look back, I see all that has been lost. The government can never compensate for what we have been through. I mean all the families, not just mine. My kids have suffered. I was never around. I missed a lot over the last twelve years. But, I figured if I could secure a land base, a future for my children and grandchildren, then that was more important than anything. I hate the way they have had to suffer, though. I have to credit Louise with a lot, she kept things going while I was on the road, at meetings and so on. Really she raised them.' (1991)

'I think [about] the main reason we are still in this fight. Basically because we understand in looking at the different Native societies across Canada, meeting our brothers and sisters, we saw that a lot of them had lost their ways. And especially in the last five years, we started realizing how lucky we are to a large degree in keeping with what we had for many, many generations. The important thing in all of this is land.

'We survived off this land for many years, and everything that we do surrounds land. For example, through our prayers and the ceremonies that we have, everything is tied back to the land. It's like a newborn baby and the attachment it has to its mother. It can't go on its own, nowadays I suppose it could. I mean, years ago, a baby that wasn't nursed by its mother wouldn't survive. If the baby was left on its own. I mean, take a couple days old baby left on its own, how long would it last? In this situation, everything that we do – for example, when a person is sick – the first thing we do is go back to the land, to see what kind of sickness this person has. Then we go back to our different areas of our traditional areas, where certain herbs are, which may help the ill person. Or if we need to go to a certain animal to heal that person. Then we have to go to the different area of that animal. So our whole territory was kind of like a drug store in one sense, a grocery store and a meat market, to try and put it in modern terms. Keeping in mind that the Creator has put us here to raise our children and grandchildren and we got to try and do what we can and hope and pray for his guidance and assistance in trying to keep this land so our children and grandchildren will have something.

'But what we saw and what we have experienced is the white priority, or oil development or governments, all they're concerned with is money. Money to them is like land to us. Those two things we cannot compare. From our ways, money never meant anything to us. That is why we are poor in one sense, in the materialistic ways. In a lot of ways we are still well off as a Native person. The two have to have a balance, as we are finding out. As long as you don't have the money, then you can't really be fighting off the powerful people all around you who are interested in more money. And yet you are trying to protect what is, in a true sense, is an inherent right to a large degree. The Creator must have put us here for a purpose. There must be a reason why we are here, to keep what we got as much as possible. Throughout this process we have been taught – for myself, my parents taught me – I got to share, share everything, not to kill anything for no reason at all. Through all these things, we got to always respect the animals and the land, and the trees, no matter what we do, they all have a purpose. As we start out in our prayers, these are the areas that you'll notice a lot of times. People are smoking their pipe; they'll start dealing with our mother, the earth. I kind of hate to use that terminology [aware of the New Age usage, we nodded] because we see a lot of this stuff, the medicines that we get off the land from the earth itself.

'When we bring our pipe around, it's all pointing to those things. Because that was the Creator's way ... and yet to try to keep that alive throughout this process. These herbs go through a certain process, like you just don't go out and pick it any time you feel like it. I'm sure that has a lot in common with your people like Henry Joe and that. Then there are trees that all have different roles, different purposes, and different medicines. It could be the root, or the pins off a spruce tree. These things all have meanings and purposes, in our connection to the earth. Same thing with the animals, like the bear is one of the powerful animals. We use that for both medicine and also many other ways. Same thing with the moose and other animals. We always had the good and bad. There is always bad on any of these given animals. The bad stuff always hits hard right away, but the good always prevails, even though at times it is a slow process. But we have found the good will always overcome that. It may be more than one thing on the good side to overcome that bad. There have been a lot of times, for example, some animals, maybe two or three animals in any given year that we didn't have. Maybe we didn't have for one or two years the moose; we had to rely heavily on the best hunters of our community to provide the meat, moose meat, for the rest of the community. It wasn't strictly that these guys were good hunters; they were backed up by medicine men who knew how to use other animals in assisting these other guys in getting animals. And we still have a lot of that stuff go on today. For example, there are times when there are a lot of white hunters around, and they are not getting anything. One of our guys can go in there and get an animal. A lot of them knew that there is more to it than just the hunter, in these situations. But that's something that we never dealt with. We only use, or do, that kind of stuff when there is a real problem. We don't do it every time someone goes out. If there is moose around, then the guys just do the hunting. A lot of these younger guys are just depending on their own luck. There is more to it than just the hunting aspect.

'Same thing with trappers. The trappers relied on medicine men a lot to do their trapping, and of course, they've always done better than everyone else. Under those circumstances, we had to go back and deal with the medicine men who then we had to help in a lot of times, when they were putting up a Tea Dance and things like that. So if I had some moose meat or duck, I would take that along and give it to the cooks that were cooking there as part of my contribution. And put in as much time as possible in putting up the ceremony. We are still trying to do that.

'For these ceremonies, that's where we bring in the herbs, to get blessed. And we ask or invite or ask the people that have gone on, our relations, for them to come and eat with us as we do these ceremonies, we ask for their help. A lot of people never bring it up. But there is a major difference between an Aboriginal person and a non-Aboriginal person, where they don't seem to have that connection, the white man. The bible, a lot of our people start believing that, that our ways are evil and they should be looking at the white man's way, which is the only way, the right way. They seem to be picking on people who aren't the brightest people and pull people in to follow. The so-called church. I think some people have started to give up hope, then these groups come in and pull them in. I think it's psychology at work. The people believe them. That is an added burden to the overall problem that exists, when you have a people that are faced with resource development. Really no way, or limited knowledge, as to how to defend themselves in the so-called political system that is in place. Or the legal system that's *not* in place by the governments of Canada.

'So [you hope] that when you are doing business, that [you] feel that everyone is honest, at both sides of the table. We were raised to respect all people and all forms of life, whether it be animal or any of the trees, all these things. So it's a hard lesson that we have had to learn through this process, whereby we found out the white man doesn't care. All they're after is money and how to make more money, with no regard to the land or animals or any life. Anything that gets in their way, they want to push aside to make way for the modern, or so-called modern, technology that benefits them. It's a head-on collision with the white society. It's something that I think we realize that we are not going to hold off forever. Yet our ways are disappearing fast. It is something that we cannot let go on, we have to try and keep as much as we can for as long as we can. Because once we lose that connection with the earth and the animals, this land around us, whatever we have survived off of for these many years, it's weakening us.

'We are in a situation where we have to keep hanging on. I think there are more and more Native people who are beginning to understand they are never going to be white. So the best thing is to try to grab back whatever they can, which is their identity as Aboriginal people. Some are even so far as not speaking their own language or knowing anything about the land or their ways altogether. It's a lot harder for them to come back. In our situation we have been fortunate enough that we have been isolated for a long time. So we are seeing our ways disappear at a rapid pace. We are also a lot further ahead in one sense than the other Native groups in Canada. But the Lubicon are fighting and, most times, fighting alone. A lot of the other Native people have a tendency to believe the government where they say we are troublemakers. But the fact of the matter is land. We are fighting for the land. There are policies and treaties, provincial legislation, whatever else other Native people have made agreements with. We are confined in many ways in what we can do, because of these other agreements already in place. So, for our traditional territory, our preference would be to hang on to our land while we are fighting with governments to try and get a settlement that would enable the people to make a living. Like, for myself, in the back of my mind, I am always looking and looking for a way around this where we don't have to deal with the government. My preference would be to tell the federal government to go to hell and keep what we got. If there is any possibility of going in that direction, that would be my first choice, looking realistically at what other Native groups got and have.

'Getting back to where I started, the spirituality of all this is that if we allow ourselves to be landless, we are nobody. Now there are differences between us and the Woodland Cree. It's more of a problem of a group of people that have given up all hope, and are on their hands and knees to the government and are more or less prepared to do what the government tells them to. Whether that be selling the rest of the people down the river, that doesn't matter to them. They want to grab onto anything that comes their way. You have to think, these people wouldn't exist or even have anything if it were not for Lubicon. With our own small group here, there are some that have given up all hope. What an Elder said about those that give up all hope is they are not any good to anyone or even themselves. So it's a situation that is happening. I don't blame anyone for being at that stage. The only thing we have to keep in mind as long as the majority of the people still want to go in this direction, then, [is that] I have to do everything I can that has been put before me.

'I am sure a lot of the other people, like the James Bay Cree, face a lot of these same problems. As we look at the social structure of any community, that's the more important thing. Once that is broke, then we have the many different problems that both Native and non-Native people face.

'In our group we have always had these family groupings, one family in one area and another in another area and so on. While we had these ceremonies, we always were able to identify where people were at fall or where they were going to be at winter. It was always kind of a government in one sense. We kept tabs on our people and what part of the territory they where going to be on in a year. For example, if there was a death in one of the families, we were able to notify people throughout the territory and track down people in areas at any given time even though we didn't have phones or anything. So we did this by dog team or horse or walking.

'The social fibre of these things [is that] older people have a whole lot of knowledge in how to survive off the land, which now is not being utilized to a large degree given the destruction of the area. Our community faces a lot of hardship because of the destruction to the wildlife. Before, one family would have a good hunter or a good trapper, some were good at drying meat, everyone had resource people in these groups. Some women were good at various things, all these resource people, but once we were pushed into this box, this community, a lot of this was pushed aside. So welfare left people at home. The older people were pushed aside, doing nothing. Then the young have nothing to do, start drinking, lots of deaths related to alcohol. The structure that held us together is falling apart. A lot of our people started losing our ways at a rapid pace. Especially the younger people, they don't show a lot of respect to the older people or to themselves even. It's a sad situation, for any community.

'Bringing it back to our ceremonies, like the Tea Dance, for example,

Tea Dance, Lubicon, 1956. Photograph courtesy of Roland Smith.

where everything that we are about is what is brought in there, into the ceremony. The people were glad to help one another. If there was a family, for example, where a woman had died and they had children, everyone would try to take a child and raise it as theirs, if the burden was too much on the mother or father. It wasn't any kind of adoption. In one sense, but no legalities. But if a father had six children and he was not capable of looking after all of them, his relations would try to help. If he had no relations, then the people would look at taking one or all of them in until they got older, then maybe he would want this one or another to come home. That was the understanding among our people.

'In these [Tea Dance] ceremonies, the herbs for medicine were brought in, a purification system and also a place where they are blessed. The structures are made of poplar and different kind of trees, each representing something different. And a certain amount of poplar is used, a certain amount of birch, willow, whatever is used. There are markings [we make] on each which are used from dyes that come from the ground. The different markings on these trees all mean different things. The lodge itself will vary from one medicine man to another. A

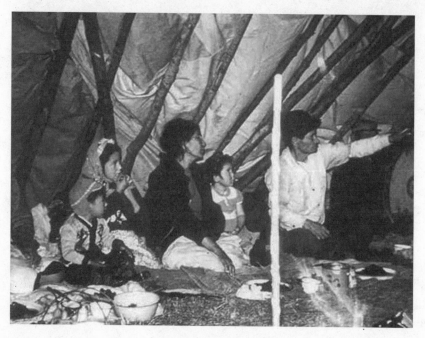

Tea Dance, 1956. Lubicon Archives.

lot will depend on the forefathers because a lot of this stuff is handed down from the years. For example, some people will have four fires and each means a certain thing. Some can go up to eight or twelve depending on what time of the year. Or two medicine men can get together and put theirs together, depending on how they agreed and if there is a lot of commonality with the two structures. There is so much that could be said about that. A lot of this stuff has meaning, like four, the four seasons, and so on.

'We pray to just about everything the Creator has provided to us. We pray to the thunder, animals. You know the animals love their young ones. For example, the bear, mother bear will die to protect her young ones. We ask for their love and their power that they have been given by the Creator. We look at them as something that has provided for the Indian person to utilize. Once you obtain the knowledge as to how you do these things for the different animals in the surrounding area, then we try to utilize those. I think that is how we have been able to survive, [by] having that knowledge in these different areas. As I pointed out

Tea Dance structure in Fish Lake, 1990.

how we use the trees, the medicines, the sun, moon, the stars, the rain, many times you will find when people pray, they pray to the four ways, and they all come from the four directions, the cycles of spring, summer, winter, and fall. These are the kind of connections that have to do with the fire, the rock, all things, things we use in ceremonies. We pray to it for its strength. For example, the rock, we pray to it for it to heal people that go into the sweat lodge. All these things. There has been talk about sweat lodges. There are many different sweat lodges, depending again on the person running the sweat lodge and who is handing it down to him. There is bear, the turtle, and so on.

'And these drums, they are passed on through generations. Like a lot of these drums that we have today are from way back. There are times when you change the hide or the skin on the drum, but the marking inside, things inside the drum, those things have to be put back and not tampered with. That's what is most important about our medicine drum, what's inside. For example, if the medicine man was helped by any of the animals or the sun or [if] people will have a tendency to be dependent on any one of God's creations, that is what their marking[s] represent on the drum. Like I have a drum and I'm not sure how far back it comes from, that drum has been handed down through the generations and that is how John got it. John's relations were also mine, our grandfathers, and he handed it down to me. And I got another from Charlie. These things you don't just pick up. Like, the ones that aren't closed aren't the same.

'Most drums will have a song that is also passed down. Or maybe the owner of the drum will dream a song and that song will be passed down. There are different pipes that have a song that go with it, like a medicine pipe will usually have a song that goes with it. They all have a way of working together for different purposes, different things. The pipe and the drum may go together for certain reasons, like a Tea Dance. You can't just sing anybody's song. The four young guys that work in the Tea Dance, they can sing some of the medicine songs because they have earned them. Also, if they need to know what does this mean, they can go to the medicine person putting up the Tea Dance like Charlie or John, and they can ask because they helped in the Tea Dance and have earned that. Many times many of the guys may go to the Tea Dance and work and not realize that they are earning the right. Like, you notice in the Tea Dance, the four guys all have different markings. One has a belt, another has a feather, all those different things mean something, most of which has to do with protection. For example, if you get into different areas where there [are] a lot of other people involved, like young guys, and they may offend someone and that can come back on them. But it won't work on them, because they are protected by these things because they are helping. The same with the pipe, you can earn the right and be handed that. Like, the pipes that I have were given to me by Elders. These Elders saw the struggle that I was in, the pressure that I was always under, so they gave me these and told me that I needed this one for protection or this one for another reason and I was to rely heavily on these pipes.

'When I light my pipe, I trust the pipe will correct my prayer, if I say something wrong, it will correct it or clear it for a prayer of strength. Any pipe here that you get from anyone, the person passing it on has to bless it before passing it on. Speak to the pipe, purify it, and as they hand it on to you, they tell you that is what it is for and how to use and to keep it. And how the different pipes have different prayers. When you're praying to a different thing, you got to use it a certain way. You don't just take the pipe and smoke it. Most will deal with the four directions and different things, mother earth, animals, spirits, grandfathers, angels, or protectors. For example, with my pipes, these animals'

Buffalo skull on fence, Little Buffalo, 1992. Photograph by Tom Hill, Woodland Cultural Centre.

spirits, the people gone on before us, you ask them to thank and pray to the Creator to share his love. The bottom line to using the pipe is how you use and what comes from here [the heart]. The bear is one of the most powerful of the four-legged animals, the buffalo, the moose. The spruce tree is our main tree, you can ask the tree for things. We use it for different medicines, the bark, the root can be used for medicine. There is a difference between the white man and the Indian.

'I think the major difference is they have been given ways and means to pray to the Creator [in an] entirely different way from the Indian people. Indian people's ways all pertain to land, while a white man has a bible and a church and that is where they do their praying. And I think there [are] some that can do a lot of different things in their church, that's their way. They seem to fall short, even when they try like hell to utilize the Indian ways. And they really take it to heart and really want to utilize it to a certain point. But with the white man, if there is a dollar to be made, he'll grab that first. Maybe that is not true of all white men, but I've yet to find one, especially within government, where how to get another dollar isn't a goal in life.

'One of the main reasons, or the way I see it in what I know, [is] that as a Native person if I want to survive and share as a Native person, the true meaning of a Native person, the way that the Creator was to provide for myself, is I have got to be as close to the land as possible. This area, what I know, the more we lose by way of land and animals, the more we lose ourselves. That is the important reason, where we know what you do within your land base, [that] you're dependent on the land. I don't see myself living a white man's way of life. I have seen some of it, have lived some of it, but you're really missing something. But when I get back, I need to go out in the bush to get my strength back.

'After all the troubled years we have had and trying to hang on, land means life to us, a way of life. We enjoyed something we are losing. For our people that is the only way. We do not desire to live in a town or city, but this is home, the only home we know. It is very important that we try to hang on to as much of our home as we can, the animals that we survived off of. If we lose all that, we have lost more than we can ever recover. Start losing your ways, then your identity and then your pride, everything else where you get to a point that comes with all that. In this community, there is great knowledge of how to survive off the land, but as long as the kind of mega-projects are taking place, that way of life isn't there. We are supposedly living in a free country where people live as they choose. It is truly an inherent right to live like this.

'I guess that is what the government saw early on, that the Native people were strong in their beliefs and spirituality, and since these were strong there wasn't much the white society could do but try and weaken the Indian through his spirituality and beliefs. When you know who you are, your culture, your traditions, no one white or Indian can take that from you. Because [when]you are strong, your mind and heart are strong, your values, your beliefs, is what gives [you] a purpose. That is why the government worked so hard to break that, to break us in that way. They get the missionaries to do their work. Now look around at our societies, the damage that is being done to our spirits, our land. I firmly believe, as long as we can hang on to our traditions or spirituality if I may use that terminology, that's the direction to go, our land and our spirituality. As long as we have one we'll be strong enough to survive this process, or attack, on our people. If they succeed in breaking us, it will be because they succeed in destroying our spirituality. It's part of my job to ensure they don't do that, they don't destroy us spiritually. If there is one thing we can rely on, as we have seen through this mess, it's our ceremonies, the grand-fathers, our Creator. We have to remember that is where the power is. The government realizes that when you know who you are, or are strong in your own identity, they [Natives] can be a powerful adversary, as history has shown us.' (1992)

John Letendre: 'I never saw a whiteman until I was sixteen.'

John Letendre is in his late forties and resides at Loon Lake, about twenty-five kilometres from Little Buffalo. He is a 'non-status' Lubicon and a cousin of Bernard's. He would often come to Little Buffalo to visit Bernard and help conduct the sweat lodge ceremonies. John is a quiet person with limited English. I immediately noticed the respectful way in which people approached him. It took some coaxing on Bernard's side to convince him to allow me to interview him. He was nervous, and I could tell he was doing this as a favour and not because he wanted to. The first interview in 1991 was more formal, and I sensed his uneasiness. On later visits to Little Buffalo, I got to know him a little better. When I felt he was at ease, I asked him for a second interview and he agreed. The first section of this interview is from the summer of 1991, the second from the summer of 1992.

'I had two fathers. One raised me, not the real one. My father, the one that raised me, I miss him. He died not long ago. He taught me everything, my mother and father. We were out in the bush a lot. I really like it out there. That's where I'd be all the time if I could. Bernard, he helped me too. I got into trouble and I was never in trouble before – well, once before, but that's not really my fault. But Bernard, he helped me that time. I shot a moose and another. I didn't do that on purpose. I shot for the one moose but it got away. But another moose behind, I got that one. When I went there to get the moose, I see the other hurt, so I did shoot it. So I had to take it, because it will die somewhere. That's not good to hurt it. I went and took the other moose, so it wouldn't be for nothing. I took them back in my truck and somebody sees that I got two moose and tell on me. I guess that is what happened, because I cut them up and gave some away. My sister, she got some of it. The police came or the game person. He said to me, "Did you have two?" I don't lie. I said, "Yes." And he wanted me to show him. So I showed him and took him over to my sister's and show him. He tell me that I broke the law, can't have two moose, only one. They took my sister's meat and some of mine. They tell me it's a thousand-dollar fine and if I don't pay I go to jail. I was really worried. I don't have any money, so I thought I was going to jail. I called Bernard that time and he said not to worry. He said he would get a lawyer and they wouldn't let that happen to me, to go to jail. He got a big lawyer from back east. O'Reilly, I think his name is. He is a good man. I don't really know what happened, except I didn't get into trouble. They gave me my moose back, but it was no good meat. That was a shame to see that meat not any good to anyone, all that trouble and money, no need for it. But that's how Bernard helps me. I told him then I would help him.

'There are people that try to change my mind, about Bernard, about being Lubicon. They say I should sign with the Loon Lake band. They start one there too now, like the Woodland Cree. They try to talk me into signing. They tell me I'll get a status card. Well, all these years now, I never have one of those. That is not really the thing to have this card. It's in your heart what you are. I know my children want one. Things come with that card, certain things I can't get and they can't. But I wait with the Lubicon and stay where I am, not change. These men have come to my door to talk to me about the band, white men. They want me to sign, they say I'll get a better home and so on. I don't like it when they come knocking to bother me about this. I want no part of what they are doing. They are doing this to hurt Lubicon. I don't think something good can come out of it when they have a bad purpose. I think they're not for the Indian. A lot of people let themselves be tricked by these white men. I wonder to myself when they talk, how come you never around before? No one cared what kind of house we had, school or offices, but now, they're all over saying how they're going to give us all these things if we sign.

'I never saw a white man until I was sixteen. I was in the bush a lot. I was scared the first time I seen one, he was there for not a good reason. That's when they tell us, you have to get a card to and pay to trap and hunt. All these years my grandfathers hunted and trapped, it's our grandfather's hunting places, now we have to register and pay? Why? Now they try to take me to jail for hunting. Trouble, always trouble when you see white people, they are coming for reasons that aren't for the good of the Indian. They run right through trap lines with the oil and roads. No one came and asked them to pay.

'Bernard, they don't like him because you can't trick him. He knows what they're up to, no good, not for the Indian, land or anything. These men here going to court now, that worries me. I don't think they are bad men, good men, I think more trouble. I told Bernard I will go to

Tea Dance, 1956. Lubicon Archives.

court with them. I don't understand a lot of what is the problem, what they say. I go just to be there for the men. That's why I don't spend as much time in the bush, where I like it the most. The bush – you're close to God, real close, not like when you're in a house, not the same. In the bush, your dreams are strong and you feel all the spirit of life around you. You don't feel that here, not really. You think that's why everyone is sick, lots of trouble, maybe? I pray a lot, I pray every day. My father, he taught me to pray, always for the good. Maybe that's what I can do to help, keep praying, all the time, asking for help. That's all I can do' (July 91).

'The Tea Dance, according to my father and mother the Tea Dance is like everything we need. Something or someone sick or our loved ones are sick, our children or our grandfathers, grandmothers, we don't like to see them die before they're very old. Every time, we see pain on our hearts or our minds where they make like crying, because our loved ones are sick. At that time, ... we see the only one we ask to stop that, is our God, that's the only one. We call him, people think we are nuts. On our hearts we call our father whenever we see pain on our hearts. The

Tea Dance we set up early spring and late in fall. That's why we are doing that, to keep our children growing up. We don't want to see them go ahead of us to die. That's what it means, the Tea Dance, to ask that our children stay with us. Sometimes, well, my father told me we can just set it up once a year, summer. But he usually set it up early spring and fall, that's what it means.

'We set it up. When we start inside there, we thank the trees that we have cut them. We broke them, because God planted them for us. The animals we thank, because we use them too. We not just go ahead and kill them, we thank them. Because he put the world here for us. All the people, they pick those things, the medicine. Those people, like they can help everyone, not just relatives. Lots of people we know just do that. But not just our children, all children, help everyone. I tell my children the bad and the good. My father always tell me, this is good, take it, this is bad, don't take it. I tell my children that. Lots of people know bad medicine and they use it. I tell everyone, like you guys, because I know you are good, you try to help. We thank you every time for coming around to our Tea Dance and sweat lodge. I am happy you enjoy the sweat. I try to do good. Whenever I get on the pipe I try to do the best I can, pray for all the people. Too bad I can't speak English very good, so people could understand my words. I have a hard time. Those people that used to know medicine, they dream; somebody tell them what to use, what it looks like and then they know. I was dreaming. When you sleep that's when you find out about this. Our father, he picked people, he knows me, I wouldn't fool somebody, I won't joke on people. I tell good people, anybody. Our father, he pick people that will do it right; he do the good work, the right things to look after these things. Same thing with medicine.

'White people don't believe. Like animals don't have spirits, every animal has spirit like us. Trees, too, just the same. Medicine in the ground, they all got spirits. Everything, every one of the animals has it, birds too. But white people just don't believe it. All the trees, all the poplar, spruce, every one of them have a spirit. Fire too. The fire is one of the important things, the fire, every one of those Tea Dances and sweat – all those things, fire go ahead of it all the time. Like the Tea Dance, we have to cook so we need fire, with a sweat we have to make fire.

'We quit about ten years ago. Those Christian people don't like that. One time they tell us we have to quit [our ceremonies]. They don't want it, they don't like, they don't want to help us. My father told me to quit on it. I talk to myself and the grandfathers. I talk to myself, just quit for a while. I ask our father, we going to quit for a while. I ask him to forgive me and forgive my children. I said to myself, "I am going to take it back in while." I said to myself. Finally, it came back now. Ten years ago this was, but I pick it up again about three, four years ago. My father was kind, he didn't want to make mad anyone.

'The drum is what they dream to make that drum and draw those things. You are not just supposed to make anything there, you dream. If you dream, someone come and give you a drum and you see the markings on it. If someone give you something like that, you never forget. And you might dream someone sings, that's when the spirits give songs. Those songs you never forget. Some songs are passed; those songs I sung the other night are all my father's songs. Indians grow with it. All was dreamed. Even the Tea Dance was dreamed. They dream these things, how to put it up. I learn from my parents, that's the way I know' (1992).

John Simon Auger: 'I don't want to let go of the past.'

John Simon Auger, also known as Simon, is in his early forties and speaks English well. I met him through the sweat lodge ceremonies, which he attended regularly. Because of his quiet nature he was not easy to get to know. He and his wife, Maggie, were always at the Tea Dances and ceremonies but were both very quiet. Maggie was more outgoing and we later became very good friends. It wasn't until 1992, when Henry Joe and his friend Beatrice and her daughter stayed with John and Maggie that he opened up to us 'Mohawks.' John Simon is cousins with John Letendre. Both are non-status Lubicon. I interviewed him shortly after a Tea Dance in the spring of 1992.

'Ever since I was young, I went to Tea Dance. We would go ride from Lubicon Lake and to Loon Lake and Marten River, we went all over on horseback. There would be about twenty of us on horseback. We went all over, the spring and the fall. We would go to three or four every spring and every fall. I can't describe how I feel about it, how I feel that today right now. That song John sang nearly made me cry. That one the other night at the Tea Dance, that song used to belong to my uncle. He raised John, that's why John got it. First, it used to be my grandfather's. I don't remember that then my uncle got it. He used to take off from here to Loon Lake early in the morning on horseback. I guess he noticed I was always working. Ever since I was about eleven or twelve.

When I started working at the last fire, that's always the one you start at, work your way up. The leader, the one that wears the sash, the first fire, he tells the rest what to do. I think we lost ours when I was about eighteen. They didn't do them as often, they quit. Like John, I never heard him sing until about two years [ago]. He's worked so long ever since he was a kid till he was in his thirties. His father quit. The songs have to be passed on. Even if you heard your father sing those songs every day and every night and you know them clear through, there is no way you can sing them unless they were passed on to you. So you can memorize it, but there would be no power to it because it wasn't passed on to you.

'So many years we did lose it, few guys can sing around here. What happened was the white man's religion came. And there was pressure on him all the time by these people. He was kind like John, he didn't like to offend anyone. So he laid off, that's what really did it. The last few years it's coming back. I can't say I really lost anything; it was really with me all this time. But nothing was passed on to me so there was nothing I could do. When I saw my uncle getting sick, there I was really worried. But then I heard John had it, so it really brought me up again. Like the other day, he thanked me for helping him. I told him I will always be here to help. I believe in it so much that I was so happy he started it up again. It was hard on him because of his real father. My uncle just raised him, he has another father. I used to work at all of the Tea Dances. Like Maggie's uncle over at Lubicon Lake and another one on this side of Loon Lake, Marten Lake, I worked in every one of them. John didn't finish that song, he was thinking of his Dad too much. It brought tears to my eyes too. We didn't have any doctors back then. When I was about six or seven, I got very sick. My mom figured I was going to die. My uncle got back from trapping. He said he was going to make me medicine. If this little guy makes it, he's going to be my partner, dreams, for the rest of my life. He was my partner. Like the drum I was carrying belong to John's real grandfather. The lead drum has been around a long, long time. He'll bring it out every now and then in the sweat but not very often.

'Like what Diashowa and what they want to do here, they say it is a changing world. I don't know. Junior here, he wants to go in the bush with me, he doesn't want to go to school. He has a twenty-two [rifle] and he is only five. I put the container on the fence; in four shots he hit it once. If he wants to learn this way, I ain't going to stop him. When hunting beaver, take everything and put it back in the water. You let things lay for a while, let it cool off, you don't just go in and cut it. And moose bones, you take them back into the bush where it's clean. Today, you see some they just throw it out the door, they aren't being taught. I teach Junior the way it was taught to me. Like the herbs we gather during the summer, the Tea Dance, we take [them] there, that's where they get their power. It was so nice a long time ago, going to Tea Dance. We didn't have all these deaths, all this sickness. Many times, I'll just sit here and think, think about all this stuff. It bothers me a lot, I don't want to let go of the past. Others seem to adapt to it easier than me. I can't seem to. I have a hard time, maybe because of what my uncle taught me. I think that's the most important thing, the Tea Dance. If we can hang on to that, that's the backbone of our people. Round Dance not as much, I hope my children will be able to sing. I remember my uncle used to sing in the morning, maybe four or five songs at sunrise. It was so nice to hear that when you wake up.

'This thing we're in now, I hope I see the day it comes. When our land claim is finally settled. I worry about my kids. What they're going to have? People just don't know what we have been put through these last years here. For the first time, I have thought we might not handle it too much longer, something got to give. Our guys here, they just drink. Wasn't like that a while back, nothing like what you see now. A lot of us wonder now, what is going to happen to the land, to our ways, hunting and things? What's there going to be left? Before, Bernard had a lot of us going all over with him. One by one, they dropped [out]. I have gone the last few times to Edmonton with him. He's at meetings that really the councillors should be looking after, but they are worn out. We worry. Can he keep going too? I just don't know. If anything happened to him, there is no one to take over. We know that here, who could do it? All the history with lawyers, support groups, band business, we'd be lost. We see the toll it's had on his life and no one here is in a hurry to step into that' (1991).

Dwight Gladue: 'Does this, a Skid [tractor] mean much more to a white man than a life?'

Dwight Gladue is in his late thirties and speaks English well. He is a band councillor and is one of the men charged with arson at the logging camp near Fish Lake. We were introduced during our short stay in the winter of 1990. The Lubicon had decided to close down the oil wells on their land, and there was friction in the community because of

Road in Little Buffalo used by oil and logging trucks, 1990.

the presence of RCMP officers. Dwight was especially upset when we talked with him because he had just lost a brother and had been interrogated by the RCMP. We grew close to his family over the years and have shared laughter and tears with them. His story is closest to my heart. The following life history consists of several interviews and notes taken between December 1991 and June 1993. I have assembled them in chronological order.

'I've been a councillor for a year now or more. These police are crawling all over the place. They're taking people in all the time, knocking on doors, dragging this one or that one off. They took Hector Whitehead in and took him to the bush, threatened 'to smoke him' if he told on them. They took away this guy's sneakers and let him go at two a.m. in this freezing weather [shaking his head]. What next? You know what really makes me mad? My brother, he died not too long ago. I knew something was wrong. I told him not to go drinking with these loggers and oil men, these whites. But he went anyway. When he didn't come home, I knew. I went looking for him. The fourth day I called the police. They didn't care. I found him. He was half in the water. I knew he didn't just die like that. I called the police. Nothing.

They took a long time to get out here just to get the body. It was awful. I had to leave him there in case something, they found something. But, they didn't even try. Do you think they went around looking for the guys he drank with or questioned anyone? They didn't care. It was only an Indian. A life, my brother's life, meant nothing to them. A life, a human life, did not concern them. But a logging skid is damaged and we have sixteen cruisers crawling all over the place, going door to door. I could not get one out here to help me with my brother. Even when he was found, they took their time – busy, they told me. Does that tell you anything? Does this, a skid, mean much more to the white man than a life? I have no respect for these people. I can't prove it, but I know these white guys killed him. I know it. But they will never get caught, never. Because the police figure they did them a favour. We have no rights up here, nothing. They can come up here, take our land, destroy us, our lives, and get rich doing it. They can do as they please and it is justified. Us, we just have to take it. Now they want to jail us, lock us up, let the rest go to the Woodland Cree or wherever and that is all legal. Their laws, I have no faith here in this system. It has shown itself to me very clearly these past years. Me, I never hurt anyone. I never kill or steal or cheat and they will try to lock me up, threaten me.

'Sometimes I just want to take my kids and go away from here. They are watching all this happen to their parents. Drinking, fighting, and people falling apart. I wonder what effect it is going to have on them. What will my children have left? There seems to be no way out. I have to try for them. I have to show them we are right and we will fight for what is right. But it has had a toll on all of us. There is so little here to offer the children. Rosanne and I try to do things, like hockey or volleyball games. We had some in cross-country running, but it got expensive. You need gas money and so on. We had to quit. The kids, they get into trouble. I don't want this to happen. But I know if there is nothing for them to do, they will drink and get into trouble. It's so frustrating. I think that is all the government wants, to watch us fall apart. Keep stalling our claim, keep logging and opening wells and watch us be destroyed by welfare and nothing to do. They want that' (1991).

Second Interview with Dwight

'I want the kids to know their traditions. I want them to speak the language. I have never been to one [Sundance] but have heard of them.

Something like our Tea Dance, but it's the Sun Dance for them. The kids need to be proud of who they are. I was raised in foster homes. My foster parents were nice, but, I missed a lot, too. I take the boys hunting and try to teach them. I also want them to stay in school, because if we get this claim we are going to need people who can handle the business. Right now, they are doing good in school, but there is nothing cultural in there. They don't learn about themselves. Mr Dewar was good. He even had the kids go down to the blockade in 1988 and write about it. The kids did well. They got rid of him and this one that is in there, I don't know. She set up a field trip to Diashowa! She isn't well liked here. The kids don't like school the way they used to.

'It's good that these young guys from Joseph Bighead have been coming up. They get our guys singing. Gordie is good, I think he picked it up fast. The boys all have drums and practise. I think that is good. I hope they stay with it. I want them involved in the Tea Dance, too. You really need those things, the sweat, and the ceremonies, to know who you are. They are excited about the Sun Dance. You're driving up with us, eh?' (1991).

Third Interview with Dwight

Not long after our summer visit, Dwight's oldest boy died of unknown causes. His death devastated the community as well as his family. Several of us from Six Nations mourned Kevin's death. We had just spent the whole summer together, all of our children playing together. His brother Timothy was stricken with grief. There are no words to describe his sorrow.

When I organized the third Drum Beat conference, a busload of Lubicon and people from Joseph Bighead attended. They stayed at Six Nations for four days. Dwight, Rosanne, and their children – Gordie, Crystal, Timothy, and Wendy – stayed with us. They were still grieving, and though I knew they needed help, I did not know what to do for them. Henry Joe wanted to hold a ceremony for them, and it was decided that during his next trip to Little Buffalo, he would conduct a ritual grieving ceremony.

With the money raised at the spring Drum Beat conference, we were able to pay for several chiefs and people from Six Nations to travel to Little Buffalo that May. Days before we left, it was dreamed that a *Feast for the Dead* was the ceremony needed; this would be conducted for the entire community. The Elders recognized that all of Little Buffalo was grieving; each family had been touched by community members who had died. This ceremony was an Iroquoian ceremony; even so, they felt that there was a spiritual reason for it – it was our people in their community. The Lubicon believed that we were there not just for research or political purposes but for reasons we might not fully understand. I left all these matters up to our leaders and spiritual guides. My job was to raise the funds needed for them to do what they wanted to do among the Lubicon. Elder Calvin Miller and Chief Arnie General stayed with Dwight and Rosanne's family. Rosanne had a newborn boy, whom they named Douglas.

The Elders did what they could to help the Gladue family. Everyone felt for them, but as Henry Joe said, 'Time is really what deep wounds need to heal. We just make sure things don't get worse.'

The upcoming trial of the men was also worrying the Gladue family. Rainy Jobin was the first to be tried in Edmonton. Dwight didn't know when he would be called to trial. He never spoke much about it. The last long discussion we had was shortly after Henry's death. I happened to be in Little Buffalo in March 1993, working for the Lubicon Women's Circle. By then Henry Joe had suffered a stroke. This upset Little Buffalo community members, as it did the people back home. I knew they had been praying for Henry Joe, and I knew how Dwight felt about the old man.

Word of his death silenced Little Buffalo. I had been staying with Jennifer Ominayak and heard the news there. I was immobilized. The chief and drummers from Joseph Bighead had stopped in Little Buffalo the previous night. It was good that we were all together when the news was delivered. Dwight wanted to come to Six Nations to attend the funeral but lacked the $1,200 it would cost to fly there. He sent Henry Joe's family a card that contained his week's wages. There was sadness throughout this time, which I would later realize was overwhelming. Trying to conduct interviews with the grieving while grieving seemed a bit insane, but it was our reality.

My next trip out was in April, and Dwight talked to me in his home late one night.

'I'm not sure where all this is going. My kids, Timothy, he has a hard time of it yet. We all do, sometimes Rosanne, sometimes me. As you can see, we don't sleep well. If you want to visit someone at three a.m., you can come here, we'll be up. It's hard too. I really miss Henry Joe. I wanted so much to go there to his funeral. It is so frustrating sometimes. It's hard to believe he is gone, that he will never be walking

through my door ready for a good meal. He did a lot for our community. Even people that didn't get to know him, feel it. It's hard. He gave
us hope, I guess. Something about that old man gave us all hope.

'I just don't know if things can get much worse. I suppose I
shouldn't say that. Maybe I will be locked up in some jail serving time!
Just in the time you have been here, you have seen how awful things
are. Sometimes it's hard. Can't sleep, thinking about all these things
gone wrong. Everyone is hurting, every house has hurt. When is it all
going to end? I think of our trip to Six Nations. Man, you guys got it
made up there. Things for kids to do, nice houses, good schools you
run. Lots of Elders and your Longhouse. I often think if I had all this, I
wouldn't leave it. People are happy out there, you see the difference,
eh? I'm sure you really don't need this, but you have been here. See,
we are just nowhere, can't plan a thing, limbo. That's so frustrating. We
are tired of this mess, tired of having been put on hold, jail held over
our heads. That's it, they are getting what they want, to just let us fall
off one by one until they did us in. You are lucky to have what you
have. I wouldn't blame you one bit if you never came back here. Why
should you? Your kids have a lot going for them over there. Someday I
pray for the day we see that here. This isn't living, it's hell. Its surviving one day at a time. Just get through another day. Hope no more bad
things happen to anyone. No bad news comes knocking at our door. It
seems like the bad are winning. You know, I have always been taught
that the good win, but right now from where I see things, the bad are
winning. The bad ones do as they please and don't even hide it. The
ones who don't hurt anyone are the ones getting it from all sides. I
can't ignore what I have seen the last years here, the bad are winning.
Us, we just keep taking it while we are walked on. I know you can't get
down to their level. But it's sure hard sometimes to just keep taking it'
(1993).

Walter Whitehead: 'This here, these ceremonies, this is where the real power is.'

When I first visited Little Buffalo in October 1989, one of the first people the chief introduced me to was Walter Whitehead. Walter had been
chief before Bernard and was now a band councillor. Bernard insisted
that I interview Walter, who 'knows a lot about this whole thing.'
Walter sat behind a desk in one of the four rooms in the band council
office. When I asked him if he would speak to me, he sighed without

Walter in Fish Lake, 1990.

answering. He did not want to be interviewed. I went back to Bernard's office and said, 'Walter does not want to talk.' 'Get him to talk,' Bernard replied. 'He will. It's just that he hasn't gotten over the deaths of his two children and he needs to open up and talk.' Reluctantly I knocked on his door and went in. He sighed again and sat back in his chair. I joked that I was under strict orders to make him talk. He made it very difficult for me, not answering many of my questions. He did say that he had been chief for five years but resigned in 1975. At that time, there was no band council and only 9 per cent of the Lubicon received social assistance, mainly the older ones. It was Walter who had laid the groundwork for the land claim. He had undertaken a census and had joined the Isolated Communities Board. He had recruited Bernard as band councillor and later as chief.

I felt like an invader, yet Bernard seemed to want this, and I trusted his judgment. Walter, staring at the floor and speaking very quietly, began.

'You know, we lost six Lubicon teenagers on their way home from Peace River. A logging truck pulled out in front of them. The car went up in flames. All six were killed, everyone in this community lost a

Drum Beat Conference, 1990. Social dancing, Six Nations Community Hall.

cousin ... a sister ... a nephew ... We're all related ... I lost my two kids.'

I was angry with Bernard. Why had he set me up? Why would he do this to either of us? How dare I impose myself on this man? I felt horrible, but not nearly as bad as Walter. Looking back, I know now why Bernard did what he did. Something happened that day with Walter: he knew that I knew, and that was all that was needed.

Over the years, Walter opened up to me. When he attended the first Drum Beat conference, held at McMaster and Six Nations in April 1990, he camped at our house. He seemed to laughing more. The last evening, the leaders and spiritual advisers decided that all the guests should return in the morning to hold a ceremony. During this ceremony, Walter stood in the circle of Elders and spiritual leaders. When it was over, he told me, 'You know, for the first time in years, I saw my children's faces. For a long time I could not see them, maybe to stop the pain, but I saw them clear as day when we stood there.'

Walter always attended the ceremonies held at Little Buffalo and Fish Lake. One time in 1990, he turned to me during a sweat lodge at Fish Lake and said, 'This here, these ceremonies, this is where the real power is. The government don't like it, they can't control us. When you follow your traditions, you'll die for your beliefs. They are afraid of that kind of strength, you know. They don't want us to be strong.'

The following summer I saw him carrying his father, Albert, out of his cabin in Fish Lake. As if he were holding a child, he carried him to the lake. I walked to the hill and saw them sitting there quietly. I thought it best not to disturb them. I knew that Albert's illness saddened Walter. He cared for him, which was a difficult task since Walter was also responsible for thirty-three grandchildren. I remembered how Walter had once carried Albert into the Tea Dance and placed him down beside the drummers. Albert's condition grew worse, and Walter was forced to place him in an old-age home in Peace River. This greatly saddened him, but, as he said, 'I can't give him the around-the-clock attention he needs and be running around dealing with court.' He would often visit his father in Peace River. By then I had already interviewed him about the trial and the court case. It was in January 1991, and we were in Edmonton, and he agreed to talk about it. Walter and his two sons, Hector and George, had been charged with arson.

'It doesn't bother me. They can drag me off to jail and lock me up and throw away the key. I have many children and grandchildren, they keep going even if I am locked up. They can lock up my boys and still I have grandchildren that will carry on the fight. They're not aware of that, I guess. I am not afraid to go to jail. I'll eat and sleep, even maybe get some rest [laughs]. I have lost too much in this to give up now. My grandchildren are always sick, everyone sick. Not the way it used to be around here. We have to stay together. That's what they want, for us to fight one another, point fingers. This Woodland Cree, what they got? Their children will not be bragging about how their parents fought for them, the land. They will have to live with what they did. Their children will have to hang their heads when someone says, "Who are you, Woodland Cree?" What is that? A government white term, not identity. Those children will pay for what their parents done. They will have nothing, no land, no money, no future. The way that deal is, no rights. They can't take it back to court, it's a one-time sell-out of rights. No title to land. That's real bad. Everyone got their status cards through Bill C-31, no aboriginal title. They sold out their children's future. I will never do that. I will never sell out. I would rather have my children and grandchildren see me go to jail for standing for their rights. They will not hang their heads over what I have done.

'I will always be Lubicon, like my father and grandfathers will never sell out. They can offer me anything, I will not sell out who I am. And I am not about to watch them destroy the land we love. Call it what you will, if you get lost, take up white man's ways, religion, then you are pickings for these government officials, you'll sell out because your beliefs are not Lubicon. That is why it is so important to keep the ceremonies going, keep the traditional ways, the songs. All these things keep us knowing who we are, pride. Government can't shake it, but now we have our own people turning Pentecostal or whatever. That will weaken them and it will weaken us. But, as long as I stay with the traditions, Lubicon, they will never wipe us out. They can't. Because we'll never say we're something else, even till maybe there's only a handful of us. [I will] never say it, never say I'm something else.

'The police were so mad. They pulled me off the road, put me in their cruiser. I smiled at them and said, "How you doing today?" They were saying everything. They were trying to get me to say something. I told them, "I got nothing to say to you people. Go ahead, lock me up, throw away the key, my kids too, then you deal with my grandchildren" [smiling]. They didn't like that! Hector, they took him to the bush. They slapped him and really tried to shake him up. They even told him they would shoot him if he told on how they slapped him around. He told on them right away. They wouldn't let him see the lawyer. But, maybe they're shaking us up, but they will pay for it later. I ask you, who is the criminal here? What have we done that is wrong? They came and took our land, our trees, our oil, we have no way of hunting, our living is gone. We are all on welfare while the white's pockets are lined in gold. They treat us like we're not human, no respect for land, animals, trees, no respect for life. They have no respect even for each other. But we are the bad guys, we're on trial, we're going to jail. For what?

'The courts, they're as bad as the rest. I had dealings with them during the land claim. They are just as crooked. This Judge Moore was an ex-lawyer for Petro-Canada. He threw our case out – even put in retroactive legislation to undermine the caveat we filed to stop the oil development. They changed laws right in the middle of our case! What kind of laws are in place here? Laws for the white man, not for the Indian. The only law I know is the Creator's laws. Only he can judge me, not these people. They will try their best to do me in. What you think the court's going to do now? They will try to hang us. They're the government's right arm. I've seen it a long time now. I couldn't be chief because I saw too much of it. Bernard was more suited for it. I watched them lie, cheat, steal – smiling the whole time. In the meantime, we have mouths to feed, families to look after. They keep us spinning. Coming in from all directions, hitting us this way, that way [sighs].

'I just wish my father could live to see the day we get our claim. The Elders who trained us are all sick or dying out. It hurts me that these old ones go to their grave without seeing their children and grandchildren getting a fair deal, a future. They go to the grave saddened. I pray that I live to see that day. I bet they don't like you Mohawks here [chuckles]. You people give them a hard time too. It's good for us to stick together. We all have the same beliefs really, don't we? White man don't want that, for us to really get together, in a real way, like how we are now with you people and Ernest and them. They are watching. It's good that the old man came too. Henry is a good man. We need people to watch this, so they can't get away with it all the time without people reporting what they are doing. Some day maybe, we all celebrate. That would be a good day, celebration instead of thinking it's a good day to die [laughs].'

Elder Albert Laboucon: 'I think they're trying to wipe us out now.'

I met Albert Laboucon during my second trip to Little Buffalo in December 1989. Bernard had taken us up to Fish Lake, where Summer Joe and his brother Albert had a cabin not too far from Bernard's. Both were in their seventies and only spoke Cree. Bernard translated for me. I asked Albert to tell me about himself, and for his thoughts on the land claim. His answers were short and often direct.

'I was raised in the bush, trapping, hunting, a hard life but a good one. There has been much change. No more animals, no wildlife, everything is disappearing, our ways are. They came in with the road and destroyed everything in their path. They cut right through trap lines, right through everything. Everything is dirty, water and animals are not so clean. I want the children, grandchildren, to have something, that's why I stay with it. I think they are trying to wipe us out now. I never thought that really before – to wipe us out. They are, no deal, just get us out of the way. They are greedy, greed like we don't know. There is nothing for me, just doing this for my grandchildren now.

'The Woodland Cree, I knew them since they were this high [by his hip]. We feed them, help one another, it's hard to believe that these people can forget who they are. If I ever get that stupid I will pay some young boy ten dollars to shoot me. This has been going on long time, since I was young. I thought it would be all okay; we get our reserve, no big deal. They seem to want to wipe us out instead, don't know why. I think they have money, no word for the money they have. We don't want much. So, I don't understand why they need to go and try to build a new band with our members. Don't make sense. A lot they do doesn't make sense, destroying the land, water, air. No matter, they think they're above all this – they're not. They're needing air, water, food, and they can't see what will happen to us will happen to them too. They don't think about their children either. What will these young ones have to drink if all the water is no good? Maybe if we keep hollering they will hear us, maybe if we keep making enough noise. It's good that other Indians like you come here and help. We need to help one another the way the Creator intended. I feel better when there are other Indians helping.'

I asked Albert what he wanted me to take back to my people, what to tell them from him. He sat quietly for a long time and then said in Cree, 'We should put our voices together, our drum, it will be heard across the country.' He said something to Bernard and proceeded to take out a root they burn before drumming. His drum was in a white cloth hanging above the bed. A blanket was placed on the floor, and he kneeled down and held the drum close to his face. He sang for a while and then put it away. He said, 'They will hear that, take that to them.' To say the least, the Drum Beat conferences were inspired by Albert. The first Drum Beat was held the following spring.

Elder Edward Laboucon: 'What my father told was like an instruction book. Because I listened, I am wiser now.'

Edward Laboucon, Albert's brother, was one of the first Elders I spoke with in Little Buffalo during my first trip there in October 1989. I wanted to speak with him because, prior to my meeting the chief at McMaster, I had dreamed of an Elder who looked a whole lot like Edward. In the dream, the old man invited me to visit. When I saw the video *Our Land Our Life*, in which Edward appeared, I knew that I would visit this Elder.

When I arrived in Little Buffalo I was told that Edward was in the bush. I informed the chief that I had driven a very long way to meet this Elder. The next day, Steve Nosky picked us up and we went looking for Edward in the bush. We didn't find him, but I was told he knew we were looking for him. Three days later we found him. I will never

Josephine and Edward Laboucon, 1991.

forget the moment. We had been driving down muddy paths for more than an hour. There were pieces of red cloth tied to bushes, which were markers put there for us to follow. Finally we came to a clearing and sat and waited. After half an hour, off in the distance, we saw a horse and wagon apporaching us with a tall, white-haired man driving. He greeted us, and we made a fire and sat on bales. Steve translated for us. I had bought a gift – a carved stone false face. I told him it would bring him luck. He said, 'Twelve moose?'

'I heard this pretty Mohawk woman was looking for me [laughs]. What took you so long? [laughs harder]. I thought I better go see for myself. I have spoken to many people. I have gone over the big water [to Europe]. Told our story everywhere people would listen. But this is good, in our bush, to tell the story. We have been here a long, long time. We have been here in this place, according to my grandfather, five generations. Indians were at war, so we moved to this place around Lubicon Lake. There was French here too for a while. They brought diseases with them. When I was a little boy there was many of us. We camped this lake here, the French around too. They brought many illnesses. Half our people died that summer. I do not want to talk about that, though. It is too painful to remember ... my mother ... my sisters ... they died then. They brought war with them too, the French. Whites always want things, they want all that is under this earth, all that is on top. That includes the Indian. They will not rest until everything is destroyed, especially the Indian.

'Today, things are bad too, only alcohol is killing our people now. Young ones, they don't listen, I tell them and they walk away in disrespect. I stayed with my father all my life, he told me what to do and what not to do. What my father told me was like an instruction book. Because I listened, now I am wiser. This thing with our land, we have been trying to get the government to settle this. We have been waiting since I was a young man. They came, they said, 'Okay, now you will have a reserve. You will get twine, flour, sugar, ammunition, and nails for a house.' I have been waiting a long time for these nails. But I think the whites they don't know how to speak truthfully, the government [laughs]. Why should I wait for this people to tell us we have land, we are Indians? Lubicon. They put some of our people who went to find out about the supplies on another band list. Of course they don't know what list, they don't speak English. So today, the younger speak English and know now what is going on. And they say we are not Lubicon, we are this or that. Bernard must deal with that. Here, we know who we are and that this is ours.

'Well, we have made some strides. The blockade was good, it got us a deal with the [provincial] people. But, now I don't know, it doesn't look so good. I am becoming worried now, everything seems to be falling apart. The people here, not very good, sick, alcohol, babies, and we need to settle this thing. I am worried about all of it. The blockade did some good. But, it harmed us, too. We got our hopes up, we celebrated, and now nothing but things worse. The oil [wells] they cropping up everywhere. They chase all the animals away. Hunting is bad too. I haven't caught a moose in a very long time. We [were] healthy for a while, lots of moose to eat. Now only the food in the store and I don't like it.'

3 The Lubicon Lake Nation Women

A Bundle of Voices

> Through all the centuries of war and death and cultural and psychic destruction we have endured, the women who raise the children and tend the fires, who pass along tales and traditions, who weep and bury the dead, and who never forget ... We survive war and conquest; we survive colonization, acculturation, assimilation; we survive beatings, rape, starvation, mutilation, sterilization, abandonment, neglect, death of our children, our loved ones, and destruction of our land, our homes, our past and our future. We survive, and we do more than survive. We bond, we care, we fight, we teach, we nurse, we bear, we feed, we earn, we laugh, we love, we hang in there, no matter what. (Gunn Allen 1986, 50)

All too often, Aboriginal women are excluded from the anthropological literature on the basis of gender. They often have a lot to say, yet they are rarely asked. Male researchers often write that they consider it inappropriate to interact with women; that is the rationale they offer for excluding their experiences. At most, these men provide a footnote or two about their observations on women's work roles, and leave it at that. It is my belief that if you include only one gender, your research is severely faulty or sexist. Aboriginal women have a multidude of experiences that men do not. As I discussed in the opening chapter, we Aboriginal women have borne the brunt of colonialism's legacy. State-enacted policies have robbed us of the most fundamental human right enjoyed by all – the right to our own babies, our own children. Through the Indian Act, we were stripped of our authority and our identity; our own children were ripped from our arms to be raised in

The Lubicon Women's Circle meeting, Little Buffalo, 1992.

residential schools, where they suffered in every conceivable way. The mothers left behind suffered their own hell; our children are our power, and that power has been stolen. Through the Canada Welfare Act of 1960, more than 15,000 children were abducted from their mothers to be adopted out to any country willing to pay (Fournier and Crey 1997). Linda Smith (1999, 12) has stated that 'in positioning myself as an indigenous women, I am claiming a genealogical, cultural and political set of experiences ... It is through my grandmother that my sense became firmly grounded.'

In Canada, missionization and forced assimilation policies have shifted the position of Indigenous women. Once respected authorities, women are now subordinate. Representations of Indigenous women in Western literature are dense with patriarchal and sexist ideologies. To address these issues, Aboriginal women authors have today adopted a holistic framework, one that acknowledges how history has ignored the massive losses that the women have experienced – losses that have resulted in 'historical trauma' (Brave Heart and DeBruyn 1998). Indigenous women are now participating in the development of a discourse based on their unique experience, identity, diversity, and aspirations.

Over the years, Euro-Canadian historians and anthropologists have represented Indigenous women 'victims' and as passive recipients of domination (Van Kirk 1980). Today, the literature being written by Indigenous women is outlining issues such as women's spirituality and ways they apply their traditional teachings to improve the quality of life, both for individuals and for the collective. This is in contrast to Western feminism, which has long sought to deconstruct traditional European views of women as a means of empowerment. Unlike Western women, many Aboriginal women had power traditionally. But their power was deliberately suppressed by missionaries and governments, who thought it ridiculous and even primitive for women to hold such authority (Anderson 2000; Durkheim 1933; Gunn Allen 1986). The father of modern sociology, Emile Durkheim (1933, 58), noted this authority in the early twentieth century:

> The further we look into the past, the smaller becomes this difference between man and woman. The women of past days were not at all the weak creature – that she has become with progress of morality ... These anatomical resemblances are accompanied by functional resemblances. In the same societies female functions are not very clearly distinguished from male. Rather, the two sexes lead almost the same existence. There is even now a very great number of savage people where the woman mingle in political life. That has been observed especially in the Indian tribes of America, such as the Iroquois, the Natchez; in Hawaii she participates in myriad ways in the men's lives.

Eurocentric representations of Aboriginal women were a consequence of Western abhorrence of the 'savagery' of Indigenous women – an abhorrence that led to projects to assimilate them according to patriarchal and Christian norms of femininity. One cannot present the Lubicon women without examining women and colonialism.

Indigenous women's discourse establishes Indigenous women's knowledge as a systematic and valid way of knowing rooted in the spirituality of Indigenous cultures. This discourse is often taught by grandmothers. It is our grandmothers who show us that all things in the universe are interdependent and that our womanhood must therefore be tied to all aspects of our way of life. Indigenous epistemology incorporates 'mind, body, and spirit' as distinct entities in search of balance. For example, physical interactions with the environment may be spiritually healing, and ceremonies are physical acts of dancing, praying, and singing. These physical acts are part of the entire spectrum of consciousness. Contrast this with Western epistemology, which sharply separates science or knowledge from feelings, spiritual beliefs, and emotions. In fact, Western science conceptualizes emotions as irrational and subjective. When women are perceived as emotional, it follows that they cannot have a place in science (Martin-Hill 1995; Deloria 1994).

So what does this have to do with the Lubicon women? Everything. The bond shared by Indigenous women rests not only in their collective colonial experience but also in their spirituality, which is rooted in a consciousness and rationality that empowers all Indigenous women. Aboriginal women's concepts of power differ from those of the West. By extension, so do their notions of powerlessness. In 'our' arenas, to be powerless is to be without your family, to be without knowledge of 'who you are.' Western cultures claim an objective rationality – a claim that Indigenous scholars consider one of the greatest myths constructed by non-Native scholars. Western claims that only scientists can be objective reflect an arrogance that can only lead to hollow understandings and ongoing false constructions of Indigenous people.

What Westerners always miss is that Indigenous women are central to their cultures. As Davis points out, the minute a mother can no longer sing a lullaby to her baby in her own language, that culture begins to die (Davis 2000). Women's roles are pivotal to an Indigenous people's cultural survival. Kim Anderson (2000) states:

It may seem incredible that this territory we know as Canada once hosted societies that afforded significant political power to those currently most marginalized: older women ... For the first time in our history, our women found themselves on the margins, in ghettos of the evolving culture. The exclusion of our women from decision-making in important political and community matters not only disempowered the women, it also disempowered Indigenous cultures ... As the church replaced Native spirituality and became a powerful agent in the structure of Indigenous communities, Native women's loss of both political and spiritual authority was achieved ... Through colonization and the work of missionaries, women were excluded from and handed a marginal role.

Women were long considered the bearers of their culture, the keepers of the sacred bundles. The Lakota tale of Tapa Wanka Yap reveals a great deal about Indigenous rituals and female energy. Holy man Black Elk (in Brown 1953,133) tells the story:

> Moves Walking then picked up the painted ball and handed it to the young girl, telling her to stand and to hold it in her left hand and raise her right hand up to the heavens. Moves Walking then began to pray, holding the pipe in his left hand, and holding his right hand up to the heavens.
>
> 'O Grandfather, Wakan Tanka, Father, Wakan Tanka, behold Rattling Hail Woman, who stands here holding the universe in her hand ... She sees her generations to come and the tree of life at the center. She sees the sacred path.'

The point of this story is that woman is the central energy of the universe. It is women who have the ability to give life. The earth and the universe are interconnected, and women hold the life force that binds them.

The Sacred Bundles We Carry

As Aboriginal women, we are tied to our grandmothers. They are our spiritual guides, teachers, mentors, and healers. A grandmother's power is different from a grandfather's, especially when it comes to welcoming children into this world. Birthing is a spiritual experience and is sacred in many Aboriginal cultures. Women are spiritually connected to their unborn and often connect with the unborn spirit through dreams and visions. The moment of birth is a sacred one that requires a careful ritual involving the umbilical cord, the afterbirth, and the cowl (the presence of which signifies that the child is an old soul returning and will be a seer or healer). The Lubicon, Maya, Navajo, Iroquois, Lakota, and other tribes all express the ritual differently, and their interpretations of the various moments of birthing also differ, but all agree that woman's ability to give birth has a sacred and spiritual significance, Meili 1992; Pierre and Long Soldier 1995).

The ability to give life endows women with the experience of carrying another human being within and knowing that two hearts are beating as one. The spiritual relationship that a woman shares with her unborn child weaves them together and both to the cosmos. For the Cree people, medicine is represented by the powers of the female bear. She will protect her cubs at all costs and is willing to fight and die for

'Sweetie' and baby Dawn, Little Buffalo, 1992.

her cubs; in the same way, we want our children to live and will ensure at all costs that they do. For many Indigenous women, the costs have been unspeakable. Aboriginal women share a host of experiences and processes that Aboriginal men do not (Green 1998; Gunn Allen 1986; Monture-Angus 1995).

The impact of the missionaries, the residential schools, the Indian Act, and internalized colonialism on several generations of women has been severe. The destruction has been social, political, and economic as well as spiritual. The authority and esteem positions that Aboriginal women once enjoyed have been severely undermined. Indigenous women are now seeking ways to rebuild their families and take back their traditional positions (Alfred 1999; Anderson 2000; Gunn Allen 1986).

Maureen Lux (2001) cites numerous historical records documenting the traditional medicinal knowledge that women practised in Plains cultures. She quotes (ibid., 76) an account of a Blackfoot ceremony written by McClintock in the 1890s: 'Ekitowaki began to brew herbs from her medicine pouch, and while purifying herself with incense, beseeched the bison spirit to help her find the source of the disease ... Her fingers danced over Stuyimi's body until she announced the ill-

ness was in his chest ... she danced in imitation of the bison.' Lux discusses the spiritual nature of healing in Plains cultures. One Blackfoot
woman, Last Calf, contracted tuberculosis and dreamed of a cure. She
was instructed to boil the pitch of the lodgepole pine and drink the
brew. It is recorded that she vomited profusely until her chest was
cleared. Last Calf's remedy was widely embraced for tubercular
cough. Lux also elaborates on the high social standing of Plains midwives and how they performed not only prenatal care but also post-
natal care for months for the woman and her child.

Carter (1996) elaborates on the traditional medicinal knowledge of
prairie Aboriginal women. The accounts of local doctors and writers
from that time suggest that medical doctors often resorted to traditional midwives and healers. Carter (ibid., 62) cites a number of examples of Indigenous women assisting medical doctors at the childbed,
be it Native or non-Native; the same women also administered brews
for jaundice and other ailments. She also notes that Aboriginal women
were marginalized both formally and informally in the legal, social,
and economic spheres. Colonialism's impact on Indigenous women's
roles in ceremonies and traditional medicine has yet to be addressed
directly by either historians or anthropologists (Smith 1999; Anderson
2000; Dei, Hall, and Rosenberg 2000). But it can be said that in every
conceivable way – spiritually, physically, economically, and politically
– women have always been central to the keeping of Indigenous
Knowledge.

The Lubicon Cree women are members of a hunting people whose
traditions are intact but who are threatened by modernity and the con-
comitant erosion of women's authority. Anthropologists' focus on the
male activity of hunting is tied directly to European cultural values,
which posit that men's labour is more importent than women's labour.
Here, the male anthropologist cannot help but favour a version of his
'ancestral' self as hunter and to percieve what women do as irrelevant.
It is women who gather the main subsistence foods and who prepare
all the clothing and materials needed for survival. Yet these activities
are portrayed as menial compared to hunting.

The knowledge that women are maintaining for Indigenous cultures
is entirely relevant to those cultures' ongoing survival. Their knowledge and voice has been silenced for too long by a Eurocentric patriarchy that has degraded all women for centuries and Aboriginal women
for five hundred years. The absence of Native women's voices from the
anthropological literature is indicative of a Eurocentric tradition of

degrading women. This tradition manifests itself in ethnocentric and sexist representations of Aboriginal women. Cree women, as noted throughout Van Kirk *Many Tender Ties* (1980), were historically portrayed as 'slaves,' 'sluts' and 'beasts of burden.' Only more recently have the voices of Cree women been documented in the literature produced about them. My goal is to lift the voice of the Lubicon women and to present their knowledge in a way that shapes and directs our understanding of their history as well as their contemporary situation.

The women of the Lubicon Lake Nation exemplify the human cost of colonization, resource exploitation, and land claim struggles. It is through their experiences that the social impact of the dominant society's oppression can best be demonstrated. Yet it would be meaningless to discuss the impact of development on their social reality by resorting to a Western quantitative methodology. Better to describe the impact of development and colonial domination by letting these women tell their own life stories. There is an eerie absence of women's voices in the literature on the Lubicon, and what is not there speaks the loudest. This absence tells me that women, the life givers, have had little value accorded to them by the dominant society: their knowledge, their thoughts, and their hearts are considered irrelevant. Injustice takes many forms, but the exclusion of an entire race or gender is perhaps the worst of all possible assults. What I want here is for *you* – a young woman considering all your opportunities, a mother who loves all her children, a grandmother who loves her granddaughter, a father who loves his baby girl, sister, and mother – I want you to listen closely to the voices of Lubicon women.

Life History: Lubicon Women

They are in a war, a silent war. During a women's meeting in August 1992, Lillian Whitehead told me, 'We want you to tell our story, what we have been through, what we are fighting for. The women have been silent too long.'

One of the first women I met in Little Buffalo was Louise Ominayak. In December 1989 she was grieving the loss of her mother. Sensing her pain, I opted to stay with her instead of visiting with the chief. She had told me once that she seldom talked to 'outsiders.' I replied that women needed to talk about their experiences, along with the men. Apparently she agreed. To my surprise, she sat down one day, in December 1989, to tell me her story.

Louise Ominayak: 'I am Lubicon and I am staying Lubicon.'

'I have been raising kids ever since I can remember. My mother was sick and I had to look after eight of them. We lived in the bush. It was a hard life but a good one. I miss that, even though it was hard. I went to school for a while. Not very good at it. Bernard and I were always scrapping with other kids at school. We used to like to fight, even then [laughs]. I had to stop to look after the kids. He went on, he was smart. Me, I just know the bush. I was up at Bison Lake and my father had left, my mother was sick. His family would pass through there. He would take pity on me and stop to help. One time he just stayed. We had one tent, a horse, and all these mouths to feed. He was crazy even then to take that on! I was so glad, now I was not alone with all these children. I was only about fourteen or fifteen. But we had fun. Somehow we had fun. Can't explain it. We laughed, went places on horseback, it was my best memories. We raised all of them.

'Now, everything is upside down, nothing has been right. This land claim. He never goes to the bush anymore. I miss the bush. Out there it is so peaceful and quiet, good. It was not bad when we first lived here [in Little Buffalo]. Then one day he asked me about becoming the chief. I said, "O.K., I stay home and raise the kids while you do what you have to." I did not realize I was agreeing to give him up. I've been on my own ever since. The children miss their father so much. It was hard, especially when they were sick. That was real hard on all of us. People just don't realize how this has torn us up inside. And him, he has changed. Worried all the time, quiet. I don't know what goes on out there, where all he has been, or seen, but he thinks a lot. Me, I don't like to go on the outside. I went to Edmonton once and wanted to go home right away, too many white people. Then my home, we always have reporters, strangers in and out all the time. I just feed them and don't say much, but I listen to what they are saying. They take pictures of how the land is being torn up and all the trucks and then they leave. I often wonder what happens to all these pictures, if anyone out there is listening or seeing what is going on up here. But things just keep getting worse.

'The hardest part is my family being torn up. I don't understand how that happened. One by one, my brothers and then sisters left to go to the new band, Woodland Cree. I just can't figure that out. Why? After we raised them and helped them, now they are against us. My father has a lot to do with that. After leaving us he got jealous that Bernard raised them. But all those years ... now no one talking to one another [shaking her head slowly]. I miss my mother so much. If she were here I would ask her what to do.

'Sometimes I ask God, what is He taking everything away for? I wonder if I was bad or something, losing everything that I know and really love. Bernard says don't worry so much, just look after the kids. So I do, just keep them out of trouble. Kids wander around in the dark around here, drinking and getting into no good. Sometimes their parents are drinking and their kids are hungry; they come to the door for food. I don't let mine out after dark. It's hard, people changing, drinking and fighting. Sometimes the young people come here, a girl is hit or something. I try to help them, tell them to stay with it. That's what I am trying to do. Sometimes the drunks come here when he is gone away. One time this man, I beat him with my broom, I got him out of here. But this is not good, I miss being in the bush. My kids, they are not learning the way I wanted them to. I wish my mother was here. She could tell me what to do.'

The next time I visited Louise was more than a year later, in June 1991. She had moved to Codotte Lake and was living in a Woodland Band–owned trailer. I stopped in to visit with her, and she seemed even less happy than during my last visit. She told me she had left Little Buffalo because it was 'getting to her,' but that she would not be joining the Woodland Cree. Her brother was now the chief of the Woodland Cree and was pressuring her to sign with them. She was refusing. Edmonton reporters were seeking her out to find out whether the Lubicon chief's wife had left to sign up with the Woodland Cree. The Woodland Cree were about to vote in a plebiscite on a land claim deal. Louise told me that the Woodland band was paying up to $1,000 for people to sign with them. She also told me that 'they are fools. Their welfare money will be taken away.'

In July 1992 she stopped by Bernard's and gave me a beaded belt, barrettes, and necklaces she had been working on. She was looking well. We attended the Round Dance at the 'steel building' that evening. We had a good visit and she told me many things.

'I get to the bush a lot. I don't like it in Codotte, too much drinking. They are always after me to drink or give them money. I miss Little Buffalo. My kids want to stay here too. I needed time to sort things out in my head. People must not realize how we shared everything all these years, grew up together. They forget, I don't. They can't buy me.

The white man is trying, but they can't give me anything I want. They took all that away and they are still taking everything.

'But I need to get my life going, my own life. My brothers are nice to me now, too. I missed them and my father is not well. I tried to help him out. Boy, things are crazy. They were after me to sign up with the Woodland, but you never do that, you stay with him on that one. They just want to have me sign up so that will make headlines. After all this, why would I do what the [white man] wants? They must think I am stupid. When I wouldn't sign they wanted me out of the trailer. If I signed I would have been promised new things and money. I am Lubicon and I am going to stay Lubicon, so I had to get out of there too! That's why Trout [Lake] was good. I was left alone up there, just stayed in the bush, tanned hides and beaded. You and I, we will stay friends no matter what, right? People around here are making all kinds of rumours, but we know, don't we?'

I told her that I understood and that I didn't listen to the rumours. If anything, I admired her for the way she had held up in difficult circumstances. I was also angry about what this woman was being put through. It was through Louise's experiences that I was beginning to understand the human cost of this ordeal. The government was exploiting the human pain of individual Lubicon, sparing no one in its efforts to undermine the Lubicon land claim.

The following spring, we spoke again. Louise had moved back to Little Buffalo. She was upset because a very young baby had died in the village. She had been the first on the scene. She did not want to talk about it and said she was trying to forget what she saw. I spoke with her again that summer. She was feeling better and was about to begin a new job. The following are excerpts of those two telephone conversations.

From May 1993: 'It is good, this Women's Circle, having people doing things together again. I hope that it goes on. Maybe I will go to a few meetings and see what is going on. They have asked me to help the younger girls to bead and tan hides. Maybe, if I have time, I will. I should teach you, you don't know anything of the bush but then I can't write books either, so don't feel bad [laughs].'

From July 1993: 'I have been so busy beading for Bernard, the belt he wanted for the ceremonies [Tea Dance] and other things. He just tells me a few days before and I have to work all night on these things. Then the Horse Dance. I made the horse blankets. I worked really hard on that. It turned out so nice. I hope he doesn't need anything for a while.

Then I can work on your girl's belt and your mukluks. You should learn, but you don't have time, eh? Some people are starting to buy my work. I will send some things back with you so you can sell them for me. I am going to begin a job, my first job in my life. I will work with Virginia in the home-makers' program. I am looking forward to it.'

Over the years I also grew close to Bernard and Louise's daughter, Jennifer Ominayak. When I first met her in 1989 she was eighteen years old, and very pretty and had completed high school. She was also carrying a child. By the time of our stay in the summer of 1991, she had had a beautiful little girl, Lennett, and was carrying a second child.

It was obvious she was unhappy. Bernard asked me to speak with her because 'she is like me, she doesn't open up to anyone. I'm worried.' I tried, but she did not want to talk.

It wasn't until the summer of 1992 that she opened up and discussed her feelings. I feared for her future: she was young, smart, and energetic, and the community offered her so few opportunities. Jennifer often told me how bored she was and how little there was to look forward to in Little Buffalo. Several years later in November 1992 she agreed to an interview.

Jennifer Ominayak: 'Now I am educated but don't have a damn thing to do ... what good was it?'

'I was always sick, real sick, oh man. I don't know, I couldn't breathe. They would take me into Peace River and I wouldn't see them for a real long time, because there were no roads. It seems like I grew up in the damn places, always missing my mother and father. I remember, too, or, my mom told me about my fingers. See them? The nails don't grow on this hand. I always hide this hand. But I guess they were in the bush and it was real cold, like a blizzard. My father had left the camp and got stuck somewhere, we were running out of food and everything. So my mom carried me in the blizzard for maybe ten miles! I guess my hand got frostbite. So this old couple that my mom had went to see for food, the old man fixed my hand with our medicine. But can you imagine carrying a baby that far in the cold? Holy, my mom is tough, not like us, we are spoiled.

'But I wish I could do things like her. She can bead and everything. I remember being in the bush when we were young. Man, we had a good time riding our horses and our cousins were with us. That's when things were fun. We were like a family more then. I remember

Dawn and Jennifer Ominayak, 1992.

this one time we had to cross a river and the men were ahead of us a little bit. My cousin, she had her own horse too and the two of us were behind everyone. We were just small and I was ahead of her. She screamed and I saw the horse run ahead of me. When we looked back she was still on the saddle but no horse! Did we ever laugh. That looked so funny, her sitting in the water on the saddle. We teased her about that. That's one thing I am good at, riding horses, but I don't ride as much with the kids being so small.

'Melissa [younger sister] is lucky, she doesn't have to go to school the way I did. Dad is teaching them how to do things. She can ride good! And she goes to the cabin more with him. Erwin too, he is a good hunter. Lou doesn't have to go to school either. I wish that would have happened with me, but they wanted me to finish school. It was hard catching up all the time because I was sick. Finally, Dad and Fred took me somewhere far away to this special doctor and ever since then I haven't been so sick. But I missed a lot of learning, being sick and away from them.

'Now I am educated but don't have a damn thing to do, no work, nothing. What good was it? Maybe that is what my father figures, what good did it do me? So he is teaching the others everything. I like to write but don't know what to write about. I want to help in the land claim but don't know how to. I see my father, so tired, running all over the place and he doesn't eat right. I worry that he will get in a car accident because he is on the road all the time. What would we all do if anything ever happens to him? I can't help worrying and I am worried until I see him pull in. Then I can sleep O.K. But everyone around here is calling, worried too. It's crazy, eh, checking to see he is all right.

'I know he was mad because I was going out and partying a little bit, but it is so boring around here. I am sick of it. I get up and clean, get the babies dressed, and then what? Maybe go for a visit, but that gets tiresome after a while. No one has any money to go to the show or anything. All of us are bored and we don't know how to go in the bush. So that's why we drink. Nothing else to do here and we all know it's wrong but it's hard to have nothing to do day after day. Everyone is just waiting for the land claim because nothing will really happen around here until we get that. So, it's really the waiting and the sadness of all this. We were involved more when we were younger. Even the principal of the school was involved and let us go to the blockade and write about it. But, the province got rid of him and now we have this woman that is not very good at all. Lots of kids don't want to go to her school and she is driving everyone away. They don't teach anything about our people there or nothing! It was better when I went there and the principal was more involved. It was fun to learn, so I don't blame all these ones for dropping out. But then look at what they are doing instead, drinking. I wonder if anything will get better around here.

'I am really glad that you people keep coming here. That is the only action around, the Round Dances and those people from the Sacred Run. I miss that old man Henry, he teased everyone. When he was here it seemed as if everything was going to be all right, but when he would go it would seem as if everything was bad again. People over the years have dropped off. It seems like when I open up to someone and get to really like them they have to leave and go to their own lives, and we are left here, just lonesome. That's why I don't bother trying to get to know anyone anymore. I am afraid to lose them again and be lonely. Like you, I am getting real used to you being here and talking with you, but you will go home and I will miss you and be bored again. I miss your girls running around here already. But you already have a reserve with lots to do there. You are lucky, I don't blame you for leaving this place. I will try not to drink anymore, stay out of trouble. Maybe I will ask my father what I can do to help with the land claim again, maybe help the Women's Circle, eh, like last summer?

'That was really good when we told that guy, what's his name? Siddon, Tom Siddon, yeah, when we told him last August. He thought he was going to treat us women like dummies, like we don't know what he is up to. Oh man, I will never forget that guy's face, it was all red! He looked like he wanted to hit you. If he would have, well, we would hit him. That's when I got upset. He had no right to treat you in that way, like scold you because you had a tape recorder. I told him, didn't I? He was trying to make it look like Daddy was a liar, too ... What did he think, we never read the paper he sent? It must be hard on Daddy to meet with guys like that all the time. I know they lie, but he sat there and lied to us and that's why I think we all got so upset. I got him on the membership question, didn't I? I remember asking you and the lawyers over and over again, I knew I had it straight. Then he said membership wasn't an issue, when he stated right in that paper it was! That felt so good, to tell him what we know. I wonder if they will ever meet with us women again? Maybe not, but I still wonder why they are putting us through all of this when it is ours, our land, everyone so poor, nothing to do. Why are they doing it, do you think?'

I told her that I believed the government did not want to settle the land claim fairly because that would set a precedent in the North. She could not understand why being fair might establish a dangerous precedent. I left unable to promise her that things would ever be fair or that life would ever improve in her community. I also wondered how frustrating it must be to be young and bright with no resources to build a better place or to teach the younger people their culture. The court case was on everyone's mind, and she promised to travel to Edmonton with the Women's Circle to support Rainy Jobin, one of the men charged with arson.

Jennifer was later hired by the Women's Circle as the youth cultural program coordinator. She had the younger people involved in the Horse Dance, and the Round Dance, and she travelled with them to a Sun Dance at the Joseph Bighead Reserve during the summer of 1993.

She has recently been hired as a nurse's aid to the nurse at the Medical Services Branch. We often talk on the phone. Staying with her during my visits and spending time with her children had made us closer.

Rosanne Sowan

Rosanne Sowan is another friend I made back in 1990. She was in her thirties and was working at the Little Buffalo school as the janitor. After a new principal was hired, she quit that position. Rosanne has a quick wit and is known for her great one-liners. I visited her often and came to know her family well. We travelled together to sweat lodges, Tea Dances, and Sun Dances. She is also known as 'the cook,' and cook she can. The men putting up the ceremonies often offer her tobacco in return for her cooking. I remember being at Fish Lake and watching her cook outside on three open-fire pits. Though she had to feed one hundred people, she looked quite at ease. Jokingly, she allowed me to boil the water for the tea.

Over time, I have relied on her friendship to get me through the lonely moments. She seems sensitive to people feeling bad. She will tease and joke to try and pull a person out of a sad mood. I never formally interviewed her, but through the years made notes on our conversations. Here is her story.

'I was born over at Lubicon Lake. We lived in the bush, went to school a little bit [chuckles]. My father and mother were okay until we lost my sister. He never recovered from that. He never forgave our medicine for failing to cure her. Things got bad after that. They started to drink. At first it was just my dad, but then my mom gave up and joined him. Sometimes, me too. I married Dwight and we had kids. Things have always been tough, no money, no moose, [laughs]. I try now. The kids, they need something to do. For a couple of years we would take kids to play hockey or things like that, but it got to be too much on us, to travel with all those kids. I feel bad there is nothing for them to do. One year we went to Jasper. We had some runners [stay with us when they visited Little Buffalo].

'Things are tough, you can see that, eh? But, we survive, we help one another. Dwight is busy with council, running here and there, doing a lot of nothing [laughs]. Those men, they can't even find a moose, no wonder we don't have a land claim [laughs again]. I feel bad sometimes. I know my dad would be better if we had a land claim. These old people, they have been waiting so long, it would be nice to see them happy instead of sad all the time. The loggers, they get on my nerves the way they want all our trees. The oil companies, that stuff is making us sick.

'The water, air, everything is dirty now. What will be left for our kids? The kids, they are hurting too. A few years back when that road came here, six were killed in a car accident. My brother was one of them. Then Dwight's brother, he is really hurt over that one dying. He found him, you know. The police wouldn't even help him look for him. He found him and still the police took their time. We figure the loggers got drinking with him, did something. Now we will never know because the police are white and they won't even try to find out. But, when that camp was set on fire there were about fifteen police vehicles here knocking on our doors, pulling people out of their homes, driving away. You would think there was a murder, but when Dwight's brother was murdered, not one cop was here asking anything. These white people, I wonder how it is they work in their heads. If they try to send Dwight to jail ... I'll punch them [laughs]. Dwight never hurt anything or anyone. He is a good father, a kind and good husband. They better not try to lock him up.

'This life here, I don't know anymore. As long as nothing happens to my children, I am glad my kids are all right. But I could go and punch some of these people doing this to us.'

The following months dealt yet another terrible blow to Rosanne and her family. Her eldest son, Kevin, died in October 1991. I had come to know Kevin and his brother, Timothy. The autopsy and toxology report showed no cause of death. I did not have to be there to know how much pain Rosanne's family was in. At that time all I could do was send cards and pray for them not to give up. Rosanne was with child and gave birth to a new son, Douglas. When I arrived in the summer of 1992, I tried to talk to her as much as possible. She said very little about the death of her son. She was quiet and still in mourning. Douglas was what held her together. She and Dwight still have trouble sleeping. They miss him at night. She has become active in the Women's Circle and is second-in-command to her sister, Maggie.

Louisa Ominayak: 'We felt so bad. That was our home they bulldozed!'

Louisa Ominayak was an outspoken Elder of almost sixty (she did not know her exact age). She was born around Marten Lake, and died just two months after this interview. I had been lucky enough to meet her in the summer of 1992 and to interview her the following December. She was active in the Women's Circle, and we travelled together to Edmonton for the meeting with the Minister of Indian Affairs. I miss her robust laughter and outspokenness.

Louisa spoke fairly good English. She went to school with the priest and nuns at Marten Lake. She figured there were around seventeen families at the time she lived there. She married Jim Ominayak, and together they raised their children. They built a cabin at Marten Lake because of the school and the availability of game. This is her story.

'Ya, we were poor, had nothing. But we had wild meat, ducks, grouse, rabbit, moose, and berries. We ate, the children were poor, clothes, not much. We built that cabin, it cost us eleven dollars for the logs and we had to get a permit to build there. Then they served us papers, but we were not there, like most other families. We came back from the bush just in time. We had only been given four days' notice to get out of our house, they were gonna run everything out of there. We had to borrow a team from Whitefish to get our stove and everything out. Then, some didn't even know.

'Boy, they came in and bulldozed the whole place. We had no home. They never did pay us for our home we lost. We felt so bad. That was our home! It was nice there, quiet, no drinking, had a little school there. In Codotte [Lake] there was drinking, but not there. The government never talk about that day we all lost our homes. I never see that on the news. They never know how we felt there, watching our nice place being bulldozed. I'm still mad about that.

'I went to a convent from the time I was seven until I was fourteen. It was good there, lots to eat. They treated us nice there. That is how I can talk and write. They would send a team to Lubicon Lake. My dad, he would wait for us to return. There was about six houses there. Josie L'Hirondelle had a store there and we traded with him and got stuff there. His wife was Cree. I got out of school and got married, moved to Marten River. All my kids were born in the bush except two, Mike and Martha. I lost three, one as a baby, one in that accident.

'Joseph Laboucon used to be the chief in the fifties. He died now. I have been waiting a long time for our reserve. I wait and wait, but never nothing. They think we don't know all the oil that was at Marten where they bulldozed our homes. We know it has oil all over there. They kicked us out. They don't want to give us a damn cent for what we know is ours. They don't know how tough we are. We'll fight right to the very end. And we will tell everyone what they did to us up here. Some day they will have to own up to what they have done.

'They cry about the money, but who has all the money? Not us. I want my children to have a nice home, nice jobs and a nice place to grow up. Not welfare and drinking and no animals. We won't settle for that. What will there be for our grandchildren if we accept that deal they want us to? Welfare, poor houses, beg them for everything, that's what they want. We lived on our own and we know what is ours and what is not. They have gotten rich off our lands. What we got? Bulldozed homes, TB, and welfare. Nope, I am gonna fight along with the chief. He's smart and he won't let them rip us off, that's why we made him that, chief. So, next time I see that Siddon, I ain't gonna be so nice as I was in Edmonton. I don't have long, so I'm gonna give him a good one. They still owe me that eleven dollars, I'm gonna get it, too!'

When I returned to visit Louisa with Lubicon lawyer Ken Staroszik, she had been taken to the hospital. At the time, we heard it was just a toothache. The following month, Maggie Auger received a call that she was very ill. I was at the house at the time. She wanted Maggie and me to know that she had cancer and not long to live, but not to tell anyone. My visit was cut short because we also received news that Henry Joe had passed away. I tried to visit her on the way to the airport but we ran into a blizzard and barely made my flight on time. She died only a few weeks later. She was another Elder who never lived to see what she wanted most, a settlement.

There are many, many more stories that the ones living today and the grandmothers before them have to tell. The themes are similar: the loss of a way of life, loss of loved ones, and the summoning of strength to continue the battle. There can be few communities that have been torn apart on every level as much as that of the Lubicon. But Henry Joe told me before he died, in 1991, 'As long as the women hold together, the Nation will survive no matter what. When the women fall, so do all the people, the nation.'

Lubicon Lake Nation Women's Circle

I got along well with many of the Lubicon women of all ages, and I was often scolded for not visiting one or the other. On my visits, I always tried to see at least one member of each family group. I suggested to the women on these individual visits that we should get together and see what would happen. Our first meeting was held at the health trailer in June 1992. There were high expectations, but we needed a focal point, an agenda. The Alberta Commission of Review was going to be visiting the community later that month. When the women gathered, I asked them what they would want to say to the public. The ideas started rolling in like thunder. Two-and-a-half hours later, we had more than enough to edit into a statement. I was shocked by their anger, frustration, and outspokenness. These women had a lot to say; as Lillian Whitehead put it, 'We have been silent too long. Now we will be heard and we will make them hear us!'

The written statement that came out of that meeting was overwhelming, a condensed version of all of their pain. Each of the twenty Lubicon women read the statement and quietly signed her name. Then they chose a young woman, Rose Ominayak, to read it to the public. Several days later, we gathered at the Longhouse for the hearing. The women joked that their meeting had made the men nervous. Well, the men had reason to be nervous – I had learned more things about the men in that community than I cared to know. Now all you Indigenous women know exactly what I am talking about here. Cree women are timid? Give me a break.

There were reporters from as far away as Germany. Ed Bianchi videotaped the presentations for his new documentary. The presence of so many white people made the women nervous; this was entirely new to the community. Bernard asked the women to speak first. Rose quietly moved towards the front table. Head down, she was shaking as she read the statement. She was able to read only half of it before breaking down in tears. Everyone sat in silence while she composed herself to finish the statement:

We, the Lubicon Lake Nation, are tired. We are frustrated and angry. We feel we cannot wait another minute to have our land claim settled. Fifty years is too long. In those 50 years we have watched our land and lives be destroyed by Canadian governments and corporations. Our children are sick from drinking water that oil has spilled in. They are sick from breathing the poisoned and polluted air the pulp mill has made. We are sick from eating animals, animals that are sick from disease from poisoned plants and water. Our children have nothing – they can't breath – even that has been taken. Their culture, the bush life, has been destroyed by development. When we were young we lived in the bush – it was a good life. Now, we have no traplines, nothing to hunt. There are no jobs, no money to live a decent life. We see ourselves, our men and our children falling into despair, hopelessness, low self-esteem and drinking. Families are broken like never before. Drinking and violence rise as our spirits fall.

We live our lives in constant danger. Since the blockade we have been afraid to go certain places in town. Our sons have been beaten by white men when they say they are Lubicon. We are even afraid to say that we are what we are! The roads are dusty and dangerous to travel. The logging and oil trucks run us off sometimes. We have lost many young ones because of the horrible roads. We are not even safe in the bush. We are afraid to go into the bush because the white sports-hunters shoot at anything that moves.

We ask why? Why us? What have we done to deserve such treatment? Why can't the government settle with the Lubicon? Why have they spent so much time and energy trying to destroy us rather than deal fairly with us? What have we done, our children, our people? What wrong have we done to the outside?

We are not dogs, but we are treated like dogs. We are people just like you. We are equal. We have every right to be here. The Creator put us here in this place. We are important – our future. We have lost more than you can imagine: our way of life that we loved, our culture, our beautiful land, our health and our happiness. What else can we lose?

The Lubicon women demand an end to the physical, emotional, economic, cultural and spiritual destruction. We demand an end to the invasion and devastation to our lives. We demand an end to the government and corporation warfare with our lands and lives. We demand an end to the mockery of our Nation! We demand an end to the genocide. Hear our voice and our message – we don't know if we'll be here tomorrow.

Men and women alike listened respectfully with their heads down and tears in their eyes. The Lubicon women had broken the silence, and powerful that moment was. The response to the statement in the media was interesting. The *Edmonton Journal* headline was 'Lubicon Women – Caught in the Crossfire' (August 1992). It was suggested that the Lubicon women wanted a settlement out of desperation – that they would accept anything. The federal government responded with a letter to the editor from the Minister of Indian Affairs, Tom Siddon, which stated: 'We want to help them' (*Edmonton Journal*, August 1992). The federal government had turned the women's message on its head. The theme the minister was trying to establish was that his department sympathized with the women and hoped they would tell their chief to stop stonewalling the federal government's offer.

The women held several meetings after the commission hearings. They were outraged that the federal government was trying to blame the chief for the impasse. They asked for copies of the latest Lubicon offer, which Siddon had given the chief and the Band Council. They read through it and saw that the offers relating to membership, compensation, and community development were unsatisfactory. So they requested a meeting with Siddon. He did not respond.

The chief, along with my research committee, had organized opening ceremonies for the Longhouse for 21 to 24 August 1992. Elders, leaders, and women were invited from as far away as Six Nations and Alaska; also invited for discussions were academics, as well as the defence lawyers involved in the upcoming arson trial. The women said they would help organize the gathering. We held a series of meetings over three weeks to pull together the Sacred Fire gathering. Various families agreed to take turns cooking.

At the gathering, a sacred fire was lit inside the tipi and sweat lodge ceremonies began. Elders were present in the Longhouse as the 'technical' people discussed how they could assist the Lubicon with the arson trial and land claim. Later that evening, a feast and Round Dance was held. On the second day, an Onondaga from Six Nations, Wendy Thomas, held the first workshop for Women's Circle in Little Buffalo. There were five elderly women representing Hobbema and three representing Six Nations. The rest were Lubicon – about twenty in all.

The men were ordered out of the Longhouse while the Women's Circle workshop was conducted. It was clear that the men were not used to being excluded; they kept popping their heads in the door. Meanwhile, the drummers from Joseph Bighead were anxiously waiting to begin the evening's Round Dance.

The Lubicon women did not say much. I wondered what they thought about the healing circle facilitated by Wendy Thomas, but I didn't ask. Some of the younger women cried and left the circle. They had never shared their pain, and the women seemed emotionally drained, and I wondered how we were going to lift their spirits before the Round Dance. Just at that point, Rosanne's youngest son, Jordie, age eleven, came in and whispered to me, 'Do you ladies want me to sing you a song?' I thought he was an answer to our prayers. He stood in front of the women, held his drum, and sang (translation) 'Never, Never Leave Me.' The women all hugged him and sent for the men to begin the Round Dance. The Longhouse soon filled. People held hands and danced in a clockwise circle. Some of the visiting Elders made short speeches to the people. A young Lubicon woman, Sweetie (Eva) Calliou, brought me her new baby and honoured me by naming her Dawn Starlight. It was a good day.

During the gathering, the women decided that they wanted to attend the next meeting between Siddon and the chief. The minister had always requested meetings with the chief 'alone.' At the end of August, the women received word that the chief had been asked to meet with Siddon on 4 September in Edmonton. The women held a meeting on 1

September to decide who should attend. Two Elders, Louisa Ominayak and Josephine Laboucon, three delegates, Maggie Auger, Rose Ominayak, and Jennifer Ominayak, and I would attend. They also asked the five women Elders from Hobbema to attend for support and direction.

I drove Louisa, her daughter Rose, and Josephine to Edmonton. On the way there, Louisa said, 'This is really good. We have not been helping as much as we could. I think this should go on and the women should not quit once you are gone.' The two Elders occupied themselves watching for moose. It was not a good sign if you did not see at least one animal on the way to Edmonton; it was best if you saw a moose. Josephine spotted several foxes, which she believed to be a sign of Siddon. She said that he was going to 'be sneaky, like a fox,' and we agreed. Louisa decided, on sighting the second fox, that we were going to have to 'outfox the fox.' Josephine wanted to see a bear, but we never did.

We arrived at the West Harvest Hotel and had dinner with the Elders from Hobbema. The chief had assembled the lawyers for the upcoming trial: Bob Sachs, Terry Munro, and James O'Reilly. We had a late meeting with them to discuss the women's attempt to meet Siddon the next morning. At this late-night meeting, one of the Elders, Alice from Hobbema, stated:

> Bernard, we were happy to have visited your land this summer. We feel your land is sacred and special and understand why you want to protect that beautiful land you have. And it is good that your people they all speak their language; they know their traditions well. You must work hard to keep everything alive. We are pleased that you are respectful of the women and include them. We have some understanding of what is going on. We want to tell you and the women. We know the federal government has a plan against you and your people. We know they believe you are at the point of collapse; you're so tired, everyone knows this. The government is trying to wear you out, and they are succeeding. They believe you will fall anytime now. Many pray for you to have strength and health. They think you will not last over this court case planned for the fall. They will have you running back and forth, attending the hearings and tiring out. Then, they will send in the logging. Who will be there to stop it when all your men are on trial? Who will run your council when you are away at court all the time? They will come in and try to sign the remaining Lubicon to the Loon River Band. They expect people to sign because everything will look so bad, the men going to jail, and all will fall apart. You must know this is their plan. You women must be there to stop

this plan. Bernard will not collapse as the government hopes. The women will help. This is good.

The lawyers, Bernard, and the women all understood that this was the government's plan and resolved to do what they could to stop it. We women questioned the lawyers about some details of the agreement we did not understand. Several hours later, we went off to draft a press release in case Siddon refused to allow us to attend.

The following morning, we left to meet Siddon. When we arrived, Bernard informed us that Siddon would give us 'five minutes and no more.'

We entered the room: five Lubicon, five Elders from Hobbema, and me. Siddon greeted us, and the meeting began. I started to record the meeting but was scolded by Siddon. He told me curtly to 'put it away or leave.' The tone he used angered us, and we asked if he was afraid to have his words on tape. He responded, 'No. She didn't even ask. I don't like sneaky people.' Siddon's response upset us, and tensions were soon rising.

Maggie Auger asked Siddon why he had not directly answered the women's letter, choosing instead to reply through the media. He responded that he thought he had sent a letter to us. Maggie told him:

In the letter to the media you say you feel bad for us and that you will do everything in your power to help. You try to blame our chief for us not having a land claim deal. We don't like you trying to say it is our chief that is the problem. We have read the offer you gave us in August. It is not good. Was there not an agreement between the band and your government to hire independent cost estimators to evaluate how much a new community would cost?

Siddon responded, 'Yes, we had agreed to have independent cost estimators determine the amount of building a new village at Lubicon Lake.'

Maggie then responded, 'Then, Mr Siddon, if there was an agreement to wait for the independent cost estimators to determine the amount, how did you come up with $73 million in this deal you offered a few weeks ago when the cost estimators have yet to complete their estimation? Isn't that in itself breaking the initial agreement with the Chief?'

Siddon replied, 'I think $73 million is a large sum. In fact, it is one of the most generous offers the Lubicon ever received. You have to realize how much money that is that we are offering you. You women have said yourselves how poor you are and your living conditions. Just think, you would have running water, new schools ...'

Louisa Ominayak interjected, 'You have made billions off our land. Don't tell us that you are being generous with our own money! We are sick of playing games. You never answered Maggie! Why did you offer a deal when those men that were supposed to come up with the amount ... you didn't wait, you went ahead and put this in the media just to make it look like we are bad people. You are the ones not being fair!'

Jennifer Ominayak then added:

> That is our land, you need to get that one straight first. Our land! You are trying to make it look like we keep turning offers down, but you had an agreement with my Dad to go with the independent cost estimators and, instead, before they even finish, you are on TV saying you have a new deal for us. Now, you know who is wrong here. You're just trying to make us look bad, and we know better. Besides, you also agreed to drop the membership issue, that we would determine who is a member. Now I read this new offer and you bring up membership again, there again. You are breaking your promises. What do you have to say? Tell the truth.

Siddon replied, 'Now wait just one damn minute here. You are making me angry. There is no need to tell me to tell the truth! I came here of good will and agreed to meet with you for five minutes, and they're up!'

Louisa Ominayak then jumped to her feet and pointed at Siddon:

> You sit down! You're not going anywhere until you give us a deal! Now you said you want to settle with us. Here is your chance. Tell us you are going to give us five minutes like we are some kids or something. I have been waiting fifty years for a settlement. Your people came and bulldozed my home. You have never paid us for that. Nope, you just took all the oil in the ground and trees off the ground, now you say you are being generous when we are all losing our way of life and homes and everything. And now we finally meet you and you swear at me and this other Elder here. Don't you swear at us!'

Siddon's face turned red as he slowly sat back down. He tried to compose himself, saying, 'I didn't mean to swear, but you ladies need to show respect too.'

Maggie responded, 'You need to show respect to us if in turn you want to receive it, and you are not showing us respect. You are lying to us. Now, I will ask you again and I want an answer, not to change the subject, but an answer to my question, did you agree with the chief to have an independent cost estimator determine the amount of the land claim settlement for building a new village, yes or no?'

Siddon responded,

I realize the cost of a new village is more than even what the Lubicon's proposal suggested because of the inflation rates and so on. We took this into account. Now you must realize the $73 million is a whole lot more than the $45 million you were offered. It is quite fair and you should talk to your chief and tell him how fair it is. We cannot give you more, especially since your band has lost many members. Even taking this into account we are giving you a lot of money.

To which Maggie responded,

Siddon, you are not answering the question and I get the feeling we could sit here all day and you won't answer, so I'll tell you what you offered. You offered us a bad deal. You offered to have our people with no economic development; you charge us $10 million to pay the province for land that is already ours, so we are talking about $63 million already. You offered to build houses for so many Lubicon, but then bring this membership up again, who is allowed and not allowed to get a new house. Under this agreement I would not get one. I am not treaty, so I am not going to talk the chief into accepting a deal that would only provide for treaty holders. I am Lubicon and you cannot determine our membership for us. Secondly, this offer includes the amount for a new school and other public services that the Canadian government provides for all its citizens. So why are you charging us to build the public buildings and their operations when no other Canadian has been charged? That makes it look like you are offering a lot of money, but, really you are adding in those expenses that shouldn't be in there. When it comes down to it, the Lubicon will receive less than the $45 million offer. See we have read this carefully. I ask you, doesn't the government provide educational facilities, health facilities, and so on to the larger public? When you add this up and make it a $73 million dollar offer?

Siddon replied, 'Now understand, we are prepared to build you a beautiful community and you have nothing as it is now. This is the best deal the Lubicon ever have been offered. What do want? $100, $200 million? We are not a bank with money to give away. You have to be realistic. We don't have $200 million and the buck has to stop somewhere!'

Jennifer Ominayak looked angrily at Siddon and said, 'We never asked for $200 million. Besides, you have taken our land. Our land, not yours. You aren't giving us anything! You have taken something and made billions of dollars from it. Now you have to pay the owners, so quit saying you are giving us. Giving us! You are not giving us what was never yours to take in the first place. So what we ask for is by law, what we are entitled to, schools, health and housing.'

Maggie Auger then added, 'Siddon, you are speaking in circles, not answering anything. Now we'll ask again, why don't you wait for the cost estimators to determine the amount and work from there?'

Siddon only evaded her questions, and the discussion led nowhere. Towards the end of the meeting, I informed Siddon: 'I hope that you do not try to jail all the Lubicon men and hope the logging begins at the same time. Then sign them up to other bands. Your strategy to destroy the Lubicon overlooked one important facet, the women. And I can assure you if you try to carry out your plan, Mohawk women, Native women, all women will protest across this country. I just thought I would let you know.'

Siddon responded, 'Look here, whoever you are, Mohawk or whatever, I don't take kindly to threats.'

I said, 'Who is threatening you? I am stating a fact. It's no threat.'

The meeting lasted for more than three hours. Over the course of this time, tensions rose and Siddon practically shouted at us. Louisa Ominayak warned him once again. He evaded all of our questions and left visibly shaken. The media immediately questioned us. Maggie wearily responded, 'He swore at us, he shouted, and he lied. He is not a man of honour and we are disappointed with his answers. He talked in circles. Maybe the chief will have more luck.'

Siddon met with the chief, and we gathered at the West Harvest for dinner. Bernard told us that Siddon was shaking when he came in to meet with him. He asked, 'Who the hell is that Mohawk woman and what is she doing with your women?'

Bernard told him, 'She is a researcher and it's not her you have to worry about. You met the Lubicon women and now you know what I have to face each time I come home and report, "No deal!"'

James O'Reilly, Bob Sachs, Terry Munro, and Ken Staroszik joined us for dinner. O'Reilly, like the others, were beaming with victory. He told us women:

You can't even begin to realize what you just did in there and the impact that will have on the federal plan. Yep, you women are the Lubicon's secret weapon and they never saw it coming. Now we'll just have to wait and see what their response is. As for isolating Bernard and trying to portray him as out of sync with his people, alone and losing his people, well, you women just stomped all over that. The real problem is, Siddon and the federal government have been exposed. You did a great job and we hope you women stay together through this next while. The court case is critical to the Lubicon. If they jail the men, you women will have to take over and keep everything going. Can you do that?

We women discussed how we felt about everything and agreed to formally organize to help raise money for our group to travel, arrange speaking tours, accompany the chief on meetings, and support the men going on trial on October.

Terry Munro told us, 'The time is right for the women to ask the federal people for some money. After that ambush they are going to want to appear congenial to the women. This is perfect timing to ask for a start-up grant. I will write a proposal and set up a meeting with the regional Indian Affairs man, Ken Kirby.'

The women agreed to write the proposal with my help and to set up a meeting to request $45,000. A series of meetings were held throughout the fall of 1992. These developed into a 'women's group' that soon became active in community-level political and social issues. The women decided that they would continue to support the land claim struggle and their leaders; but they would also focus on improving the community's social well-being. They expressed concern about the 'human condition.' They felt that the community had been torn apart through years of struggle, which had led to social breakdown.

The federal government gave a 'one-time' grant of $20,000 to the Women's Circle. The money was to be used to help the women begin planning their organization's objectives. Also the Band Council signed over funds to the women through Band Council resolutions and donated $3,300 from the Brighter Futures fund.

The band's philosophy was 'hands off' the business of the Women's Circle. In October 1992 the chief and council stated: 'In pursuing a land claim for the Lubicon people, the Chief and Council has had little time to pay close attention to the social breakdown in the community. We support the women's initiative to work towards improving the community and cultural survival.'

The women met weekly. Maggie Auger provided much of the leadership. The women decided that craft gatherings would be the most comfortable environment for exchanging ideas. Eventually, they assembled these ideas and distributed them throughout the community via a one-page newsletter. Their goals and objectives, as published in the September 1992 newsletter, were as follows:

1 To help the community become stronger and work together.
2 To relearn to work collectively and help each other.
3 To help organize community meetings and gatherings.
4 To help gather ideas for recreation and other activities for the young people.
5 To educate each other about rights and land claims.
6 To bring in resource people to do workshops, training, and cultural activities such as Round Dances.
7 To raise money for the women's meetings, attend women's conferences, travel and learn about the outside, etc.
8 To start a crafts centre.
9 To offer baby-sitting services for women who attend meetings and workhops.
10 To work to support the political struggles that affect all community members. (Women's Circle Sept. 1992)

The women contacted Elaine Bishop, a Quaker who worked in the community. She was also a member of Friends of the Lubicon. Elaine, who worked with lawyers and church groups, secured a house in Edmonton for the wives, mothers, and sisters of the Lubicon men on trial. The women made plans to work with the men during their trial and to alternate women to support them while in Edmonton. The trial seemed to bring the people together again. More than this, however, it generated stress in an already shaken community.

The women's work in establishing a collective spirit was of huge importance to community healing. Continuing in this direction was of utmost importance to them. The women had laid the groundwork over the previous year for bringing the community together again; a deeper level of healing was now beginning to be addressed. This involved collective as well as individual healing.

The Women's Circle was a means for women to release their anger, frustration, despair, and fear so that hope, confidence, happiness, and empowerment could emerge. The women decided that after the trial, the circles would continue, both informally and formally. Craft circles were the informal approach. These are Lubicon women's traditional way to express themselves and support one another; during these times, they listen to one another and are listened to. They reinforce friendships and lend one another support and strength. The 'formal' approach to healing involved bringing outsiders into the community for 'talking circles,' that is, workshops and structured meetings to help the women express themselves and their feelings. The Lubicon believe that healing begins with the individual and from there moves to family and then community. Healing builds a strong nation.

Sweat lodges and spiritual ceremonies were also seen as avenues to bring the community back together. Because many of the women had adopted a Christian faith, there was some friction between the traditional and non-traditional women. In circle discussions about ceremonies, traditional ways were beginning to be redefined as cultural ways. This made it easier for Christian members to accept and participate in the cultural events. Lorraine, a Cree woman from Slave Lake and workshop facilator explained many of the traditions in a broad context so that all members could understand what they might not have understood before, such as the purpose of sweat lodge ceremonies. The Women's Circle hoped that all community members would follow Lubicon traditions in the healing process. If healing were accomplished, conflict between the two religions would weaken and healing could begin collectively.

Lubicon women have always involved themselves in the political, social, spiritual, and economic spheres of their society. The development of the Women's Circle was a result of two forces: their political struggle, and their desire to improve their conditions. They shared common experiences, but at the same time they had found themselves caught in a vicious circle of social breakdown and powerlessness. It was the women who had suffered the most as a consequence of resource development on their land and the government's colonial policies. They had an important story to tell. But only recently had they begun to share that story of human tragedy with outsiders. Many of their stories had yet to reach the public eye, and perhaps they never will (Women's Circle June 1993).

There was some speculation that the men would feel threatened by the women's group. However, the chief and council supported their work and welcomed their assistance in the public sphere. Also, the husbands of the circle leaders offered the circle strong support. Some feared that tensions would arise between the men and the women, but this did not happen. A few community members felt threatened by the circle; these women held positions of power in the community, and some Lubicon were afraid the Women's Circle was going to 'take over everything.' The women alleviated their fears to an extent by phoning them constantly and inviting them to meetings, and by disseminating the minutes of their meetings. This seemed to lessen people's anxieties.

Some of the families in Little Buffalo did not participate in the circle, for various personal reasons. By and large, though, the women represented most kinship families and were determined to repair the damage that the 'outside' had done to their personal lives, their families, and their community and nation.

As leader of the Women's Circle, Maggie Auger stated in November 1992:

Why I do this work here, stay with it, the women, is because I am afraid so much has been lost. Our Elders are passing away. They have all the knowledge. Me, I know something about tanning hides, the bush. I am willing to get the younger ones interested in doing these traditional things. We have great respect for the land, the animals, the life, the ceremonies. I don't want us to lose that, too. The younger ones must know the meaning of the drum, the songs, the pipe, honoring our ancestors, what the Elders tell us. This is how we know who we are. I don't want my kids growing up not knowing who they are, like you see so many. Then drugs, alcohol and the rest follow. Too many of our young are going that way because they aren't taught the traditions. They are losing their identity. We know the land, we know where we were born, where we gave birth to our children, where our people are buried. We remember traveling to different camps, Tea Dances. John used to travel all over with Bernard when they were young to go to ceremonies, Tea Dances. They would ride four days by horseback to attend these ceremonies. Our children will never know that life. They don't know their home so well. It is like our home, our house here and it's being taken over by outsiders, destroyed, I should say. So, I am only doing my duty as a mother and protecting what we have here, for our children, protecting our children. I see it as a traditional responsibility, even though I am doing things not so traditional like leaving my kids to go speak somewhere. It is hard at times. But it has been really hard on the men, too, so maybe we can help here and there a little bit.

As a woman I am aware of all the problems here, the miscarriages, the babies that die. We know better than anyone how this development has hurt us that the outside never sees or hears about. But, we don't normally talk of our personal tragedies, that's not our way. But truthfully, the government has done quite the job on us. Letting us hang in the air like this. Creating new bands. Tearing families apart. This has taken a toll on us and we never let anyone know how much suffering really goes on here. The Women's Circle maybe can ease our pain. Keep us together, support for one another. We must stay together and keep our ways strong. That is what I believe will get us through this.

4 Echoes from the Future and the Faces Yet to Come

Is it possible or even worthwhile to present Indigenous Knowledge to those who have always denied us our rightful place in our own homelands? It seems insanely paradoxical to have to prove to the oppressor that he is oppressing you! This book has attempted to bring a truth of ours to you.

The story of the Lubicon is filled with contradictions, extreme polarizations of existing First Nations realities, opposing truths in constant tension. The examples are numerous and varied. For example, the Minister of Indian Affairs, Bill McKnight, was responsible for settling the Lubicon land claim, yet at the same time he was pumping millions into the exploitation of those Lubicon lands. Another Minister of Indian Affairs, Tom Siddon, told to the Lubicon women, 'I honestly am here to help you, I have your best interests at heart.' Yet at the same time his department was creating dissident bands in order to destroy the Lubicon. To have to watch men like these smugly attempt to deny, degrade, and destroy you is the ultimate humiliation.

As the Lubicon have shown, if Indigenous people hope to survive they must hold on to their knowledge. From the West's perspective, Indigenous people are always standing in the way of progress, development, and civilization. As the Lubicon have demonstrated clearly, their survival depends on resistance to all three. Clearly, Indigenous people have a very different understanding of the problem.

The history of relations between Indigenous peoples and the West reflects an ongoing interplay of coexisting realities and glaring inequalities, with the dialogue always conducted in English. If we want to join the conversation, we have been expected to 'ease' ourselves as an act of submission to the powerful. We must speak their language, obey

Tea Dance, 1956. Lubicon Archives.

their rules, and never, ever change the discourse or the subject, for fear of offending the offender. In the Lubicon case, it could well be suicidal to withdraw from the conversation, however one-sided. Yet somehow, the Lubicon have had to find a way to tell their own story with their own voice.

For the Lubicon, the stakes in this dialogue are high. To retreat or accept an unacceptable deal would split apart families along Status/non-Status lines, sentence their society to welfare dependency, and allow the destruction of their land base and ultimately the fibre of their society. In accepting the colonialism, the Lubicon would be denying their world view, culture, identity, and belief system. Indigenous people around the world can identify with the Lubicon people's need to survive and with their need to resist colonialism.

By continuing to resist, they are inviting the very result they are attempting to avoid – social chaos. The Lubicon are in a war that has inflicted heavy casualties on them. The agents of Canada's power – the legal system, the corporations, the media – are highly sophisticated and well funded and have succeeded in subordinating Indigenous people so that their natural wealth can be exploited. And this power structure is global in scope. The Lubicon endure abuse and injustice on

Lubicon children riding horses, Little Buffalo, 1993.

a daily basis, as government-backed corporations strip their land of all its value and then leave.

The Lubicon know that Canada is conducting a campaign of genocide. Any attempt to destroy a people is just that: 'genocide.' Yet this truth has been shrouded in legal and economic terminology that blurs the reality of what is taking place in Little Buffalo, Alberta. The government's deliberate attempt to tear the Lubicon apart by creating two bands is 'genocide.' Why, then, do the Lubicon continue to engage in a discussion when they know that the *other side* is attempting to destroy them?

Fast-cash, quick-fix deals have long-term consequences that place Indigenous leaders in the position of having to either say 'yes' to a bad long-term deal and pay the consequences later, or say 'no' and look like bad guys in front of their own people (Jaimes 1992).

The Lubicon can continue to resist the colonization process instead of accepting the deal offered – a deal that would condemn them to slow social breakdown leading to genocide. Whether they accept it or not, the choice itself illuminates how internal colonialism and genocide continue to operate in Canada. More importantly, it reveals the Canadian government's hollow commitment to human rights and democracy.

At the time this book was going to press, Canada was still refusing to sign the UN Declaration of Human Rights, along with Colombia and Russia. It was also refusing to sign the UN Declaration on the Rights of Indigenous Peoples. On 14 September 2007, Steven Lambert wrote in the *Globe and Mail:*

> Aboriginal leaders, human rights groups and the opposition blasted the Conservative government yesterday after Canada voted against a United Nations declaration on aboriginal rights ... They accused the government of trying to sweep aside an important show of support for aboriginals that took 20 years of negotiations among UN countries ... 'By opposing this declaration, the Conservative government has signalled to aboriginal Canadians that their rights aren't worth defending,' Liberal Leader Stéphane Dion said in a statement ... The United Nations Declaration on the Rights of Indigenous Peoples passed easily yesterday, 143–4. Canada, New Zealand, Australia, and the United States voted against and 11 countries abstained. '... It wouldn't contravene laws that are in place,' NDP Indian Affairs critic Jean Crowder said from Nanaimo, B.C. 'I think [Canada's vote] is a very cowardly and, I would say, un-Canadian approach to human rights.'

At last, the world is beginning to see what we already know and live: Canada has no commitment to Indigenous peoples' human rights.

The Lubicon ideology demands an adherence to traditional values and beliefs, and these are presented in the public arena in the English language by Lubicon representatives. Fred Lennerson and James O'Reilly are the 'Lubicon public officials.' Though the two dialogues are connected, the public one is very different from the one that takes place in private. Neither Fred nor James attempts to penetrate the private, dialogue; instead, they battle in the official dominant ideological arena on behalf of the Lubicon.

In the private arena, conversations, traditions, and beliefs both form and inform Lubicon consciousness and fuel their spirit of resistance. The conversation is in Cree and touches on realities both ordinary and non-ordinary. That conversation is often with the spirit world, which offers directions to the Lubicon, who then are responsible for following those directions, having placed their faith in the Creator's power. The grandfather spirits of the Creator have handed down laws that must be respected and obeyed. The Lubicon believe that there is no power as great as the Creator's, no law above the Creator's law. There is no negotiating with natural laws – one cannot compromise with natural law. The Indigenous people who travelled to Little Buffalo reaffirmed these beliefs. Traditional Lubicon beliefs demand that the people be strong in obeying the Creator's laws. If they are, they will be protected and rewarded. The Traditional Knowledge of the Lubicon is similar to what I have been taught as a Mohawk; the discussions the Lubicon engaged in with me and Henry Joe were premised on the same values, world view, and ideology.

The system that Henry Joe refers to is an Indigenous one that has been given to the people by the Creator. Each and every nation has such a system. The systems differ in their cultural expressions, but these natural laws are universally observed and celebrated through ceremonies. Ceremonies are not solely an expression of or a reaction to domination or repression. Rather, they are expressions of ancient spiritual and cultural philosophies that reinforce the consciousness and practices of a collective system of beliefs. The Lubicon have a sophisticated way of thinking, one that accounts for all life, for creation itself, and for faces yet unborn. The Lubicon have a collective understanding of their humanity and spirituality and of its denial by their oppressors.

The Lubicon Lake Nation's women say that they are human beings expressing what the denial of humane treatment is like. They have always been disregarded, perceived as non-thinking people whose rights need not be respected. This condition can be traced back to early contact and the debates of Valladolid in 1542. Indigenous people do not need to study or debate oppression – we know what it is through experience. The Lubicon do not need to know the Geneva Convention's definition of genocide; they know what it is through their individual and collective experience. That Lubicon women ended their statement with these genuinely fearful words – 'Hear our voice ... we don't know if we'll be here tomorrow' – was not political theatre. They whispered it, heads down tearfilled and eyes (damp). Who better to explain oppression and genocide than the very people who must endure the systematic destruction of their land and their very lives?

Official versions of Lubicon history have failed to include the Lubicon themselves. Those who wrote it, wrote out the Lubicon experience, thereby missing the depth of Lubicon beliefs. In writing this book, I have had to address issues that the dominant society respects and that it expects me to cover; as a consequence, even I am nervous that readers will use what I am telling them in order to once again disrespect the people. After all, when we try to talk for ourselves, white people accuse us of interfering with their right to explain us to our-

Fish Lake, 1991. Photograph by Dawn Hill.

selves. The Lubicon people and their leaders firmly abide by their knowledge. The Lubicon are not fighting just for a land claim; they are fighting for life itself, for all of Creation, for the animals and plants, the air and water. Their past, present, and future are totally interconnected, just as the Lubicon are all connected to their place within Creation. As Bernard Ominayak pointed out, 'All of Creation can survive without us, yet we are dependent upon all Creation for our life, not just us either. Someday all these people, they will realize what we stood for.'

Deals such as the one offered to the Woodland Cree, who signed away their Aboriginal title and their right to protect the land in return for superficial benefits such as fast cash and houses, go against Lubicon logic and beliefs. Lubicon society, in resisting such deals, has been traumatized by the thoroughly demoralizing processes of colonialism and genocide.

The strength of the Lubicon people's determination to reach a fair deal is rooted in their firm belief that the good always overcomes the bad. When things may look bad, the Lubicon can always consult the Elders for advice, strength, guidance, and wisdom. In the internal arena, their struggle for cultural survival includes restructuring their damaged traditional system by recreating a modern anti-colonial community. Their goal is to re-establish traditional social, cultural, political, spiritual, and philosophical structures. The relationship the Lubicon leaders created with the Six Nations Elders was based largely on a search for Indigenous models that would strengthen traditional values and principles. In that sense, the development of a relationship with the Six Nations Confederacy was a deliberate strategy of resistance to the colonial model. The band office represented a tool of domination, which was reinforced by the fact that business there revolved mostly around handing out welfare cheques. The powerlessness the Lubicon felt in the band office inspired them to take up overt forms of resistance, such as building a Longhouse in which to conduct ceremonies, community business, and meetings with officials. The Lubicon . withdrawal from the colonial model of governance led to rumours that the Lubicon were 'falling apart.' This Conquistador thinking – as John Mohawk refers to it – fails to acknowledge the existence of an Indigenous consciousness that has long informed political, social, and economic activities. As the Lubicon have demonstrated, their spiritual knowledge guides their choices but is also a means to an end in all spheres of their existence.

Racism fuels the broader society's consent to genocide. Concepts within the dominant ideology such as survival of the fittest, manifest destiny, progress, and development have all empowered government officials to carry out their agenda with little public protest. Unfortunately, the public buys into and perpetuates the official ideology. The Lubicon are working tirelessly to save their culture, reconstruct their community, and resist genocidal colonial domination. Bernard Ominayak, while imperfect as all humans are, is a superb Native leader. He exhausts himself keeping the body and soul of the Lubicon Nation together.

What Then Must We Do?
I sit
on a
man's back
and make
him carry
me and yet assure myself and
others that I am sorry for him

and wish to lighten his load by
all possible means – except by
getting off his back
(Leo Tolstoy, 1886)

There have been no more of the massacres that our ancestors witnessed. The West's technology has become sophisticated, and so has
their destruction of innocent Indigenous populations that stand in
their way. Europeans have always honored the men who successfully
complete their agenda. Many Euro-American 'heroes' have been com-
mended for helping destroy Indigenous populations (Jaimes 1992).

Today, as we have seen with the Lubicon, the massacres are industrial,
technological, and 'white collar,' reflecting the sophistication that the
Canadian colonizers have attained. The Lubicon assaulted at the economic, legal, political, emotional, spiritual, and psychological levels,
and at times physically as well. They have withstood these attempts to
destroy them by utilizing all the democratic tools available to them as
well as their traditional sources of strength. That there has been no
actual bloodshed does not excuse Canada's ongoing efforts to destroy
them.

This research reaches far beyond Eurocentric issues of cultural survival, resistance, ethnographic authority, and voice. From what I have
witnessed and from what I know, the Lubicon want to tell us that what
they have undergone is an example of Canada's ongoing modern practice of colonialism. They are the targets of a relentless government
campaign to destroy an Indigenous people. And here the Mohawks are
in 2006 – I never thought I would be afraid to enter the town Caledonia. When Caledonia complained that the blockade was hurting its
economy, the federal government quickly doled out $1.5 million in
compensation. In other words, in only three months the townspeople
received more than the Lubicon have in ninety years, or us in two hundred. The Lubicon and Six Nations continue to negotiate in good faith
for future generations. But will the younger generations, who are 60
per cent of the population, be so patient? Would you be?

In June 1992, Bernard Ominayak summed it up:

As long as I am standing, which may not be too much longer [chuckles], I
will move in the direction given to me by the Elders. I cannot, with good
conscience, accept a deal that sentences us to a lifeless life. One cannot

know the agony of trying to keep going for reasons that others don't comprehend. If the people want to go in another direction, then they must find someone else, because I cannot accept a bad deal my grandchildren will pay for to appease a few. I'd like to go to my grave knowing I followed our ways and did the right thing. You know, it's easy to take the fast way out when you can't see the light at the end of the tunnel. When all you see is death and sickness, despair and growing social problems. But as long as we follow our ceremonies, follow those instructions that have helped us survive for thousands of years, then I know there is hope. Someday, maybe people will see that this is what it is, a white government trying to wipe out a people who are sitting on billions of dollars. From what I have heard this is what they have done since they came to this land, yet people don't want to believe it, they are afraid to say it, afraid to know that it is true. But I never talk about it, because just getting people to understand Canada breaks its own laws, uses courts to legalize their greed and so on, is more than enough. I know the truth of the matter as do the old people. They are intentionally destroying us in the hopes the Lubicon will be destroyed for good. Yet I must sit across from these bastards and deal empty deals, public affirmations for them to say, 'We tried, see, here is the records of proof.' So they can cover their ass when someone calls it for what it is, genocide. They can get jokers to feed the public their bullshit while all the time they know, we know. Hopefully the world will know what in fact Canada is doing here and has done to my people. And for that, there is no amount of compensation, no deal that can compensate the land, the animals, the water, the air, the human lives lost, marred, and destroyed. No, the white will never tell his truth because if he had one he wouldn't do all the destruction to the world he has done.

I have tried to tell our story to you in the best way I know how, in a way that both Indigenous and academic audiences will understand. I have tried to express the beauty and strength of Haudenosaunee ways and Lubicon ways to demonstrate that the value of a people, a culture, is beyond measure. I don't think it is possible for us to fail as long as we follow the original laws and bring forth what we know with a good mind and heart. The hope in our hearts comes from the Creator. Henry Joe warned, 'What happens to the Lubicon we will all follow. If they win we all win.' I wonder if he knew all the time where we would be a decade later. One of the first leaders to respond when the Six Nations were raided by the Ontario Provincial Police in April 2006 was Bernard.

On 1 May 2006, Bernard sent a letter to Jim Prentice, the Indian Affairs minister, and to David Ramsey, Ontario Minister of Natural Resources and Minister Responsible for Aboriginal Affairs, that stated,

Dear Sirs;

I have been following the situation at Caledonia with great concern.

The people of Six Nations have consistently supported our people in our efforts to protect our Traditional Territory and achieve a just settlement of our long-standing land rights dispute. The Lubicon people wish to express our solidarity with our sisters and brothers of Six Nations at Caledonia in their effort to protect their lands and resolve their longstanding land rights dispute.

Both of our peoples have stood up for our rights in a peaceful and respectful manner. We have been patient. We have tried to find ways to co-exist with your governments and with the people that surround our lands. Yet Canadian governments have used dialogue not as a means to resolve disputes but as a way of forestalling resolution while business interests steal every last thing of value from our lands.

When we challenge this duplicitous behaviour we are criminalized and attacked. Canadian courts are used to provide legal cover for the continued theft of our lands and resources. Police are sent in to break up our protests.

Yet, if Canadian governments continue to avoid negotiated resolutions to long-standing disputes, what options do we have? Should we allow corporations to destroy our lands, our livelihoods, our way of life, and to take what is rightfully ours? Should we allow governments to claim that they are sincerely seeking to resolve these disputes while they allow others to forever alter the very lands which are the subject of our disputes?

The people of Six Nations at Caledonia have decided to protect their lands before they are irreparably altered. We support them in their stand.

We ask that the governments of Ontario and Canada cooperate with the people of Six Nations at Caledonia and negotiate a just resolution of their land rights in good faith. We ask that no further attacks on their encampment by police or any other parties be allowed while the parties seek a just resolution of their land rights. And we ask that the governments of Ontario and Canada commit to a freeze on further development in areas where the rights to the land are in dispute unless the aboriginal people have provided their full consent to the activity.

Only when all parties must find a just resolution before any are allowed to advance their interests will there be any incentive to resolve the many long-standing land rights disputes which are before us.

Sincerely,
Bernard Ominayak
Chief, Lubicon Lake Indian Nation
cc The people of Six Nations at Caledonia

If it is possible to empower the people by using our voice, our networks, and our citizenship, then I call upon all people who have read this book and heard the Lubicon and who know that as of the 16 September 2007, the Lubicon still have no deal – to act. Students, churches, organizations, and political leaders, take the necessary steps to help end the ongoing destruction of a people. Contact the organization Friends of the Lubicon and offer your support to their ongoing activities to support the Lubicon. If you're still in disbelief that Canada continues to oppress Indigenous people, read the most recent 'acts' Canada carried out against Indigenous people.

On 6 September 2007, Sue Baily of Canadian Press wrote:

Canada was cast yesterday as a bad actor that aggressively campaigned alongside countries with tarnished human-rights records in its failed bid to derail the United Nations Declaration on the Rights of Indigenous Peoples ... In fact, documents released to Amnesty International under the Access to Information Act show that the government fought the declaration despite advice from its own officials in Foreign Affairs, Indian Affairs, and the National Defence, all urging its support. The declaration sets out global human rights standards for indigenous populations. Native groups, especially in developing countries, report abuse, land losses, disappearances, and even murder at the hands of governments that refuse to recognize their status or title ... Canada's strident opposition to the declaration is a 'crime' that flies in the face of Ottawa's desire to promote democracy, say Joseph Ole Simel, Co-ordinator of the African Regional Indigenous Caucus. 'It's a crime against indigenous people globally, and it's a crime against indigenous people in Canada,' he told a news conference yesterday in New York. This as Prime Minister Stephen Harper 'is trying to dictate to developing nations what they should do. Indigenous people in Canada must be going through hell.' (www.thestar.com/news/article/254160; accessed 10 Nov. 2007)

Canada joined forces with Russia and Colombia to wage a campaign against the UN Human Rights Declaration. It didn't end there: Canada campaigned as hard, if not harder, against the Declaration on the Rights of Indigenous Peoples, which passed on 13 September 2007. An Indigenous Peoples Voices Press Release, 13 September 2007, stated:

Historic Milestone for Indigenous Peoples Worldwide as UN Adopts Rights Declaration

Marking a historic achievement for the more than 370 million indigenous peoples worldwide, the General Assembly today adopted the Declaration on the Rights of Indigenous Peoples, the result of more than two decades of consultation and dialogue among governments and indigenous peoples from all regions.

'Today, by adopting the declaration we are making further progress to improve the situation of indigenous peoples around the world,' stated General Assembly President Haya Al Khalifa.

'We are also taking another major step forward towards the promotion and protection of human rights and fundamental freedoms for all.'

Secretary-General Ban Ki-moon warmly welcomed the adoption, calling it 'a triumph for indigenous peoples around the world.'

He further noted that 'this marks a historic moment when UN Member States and indigenous peoples reconciled with their painful histories and resolved to move forward together on the path of human rights, justice and development for all.'

Adopted by the Human Rights Council in June 2006, the Declaration emphasizes the rights of indigenous peoples to maintain and strengthen their own institutions, cultures, and traditions and to pursue their development in keeping with their own needs and aspirations. It establishes an important standard for eliminating human rights violations against indigenous peoples worldwide and for combating discrimination and marginalization.

'The 13th of September 2007 will be remembered as an international human rights day for the Indigenous Peoples of the world, a day that the United Nations and its Member States, together with Indigenous Peoples, reconciled with past painful histories and decided to march into the future on the path of human rights,' said Ms Vicky Tauli-Corpuz, Chairperson of the UN Permanent Forum on Indigenous Issues.

The Declaration addresses both individual and collective rights, cultural rights and identity, rights to education, health, employment, language, and others. The Declaration explicitly encourages harmonious and cooperative relations between States and Indigenous Peoples. It prohibits discrimination against indigenous peoples and promotes their full and effective participation in all matters that concern them.

Calling the Declaration 'tangible proof of the increasing cooperation of States, Indigenous Peoples and the international community as a whole for the promotion and protection of the human rights of indigenous peoples,' Under-Secretary-General for Economic and Social Affairs, Mr Sha Zukang, said that the UN 'has fulfilled its role as the world's parliament and has responded to the trust that Indigenous Peoples around the world placed in it, that it will stand for dignity and justice, development and peace for all, without discrimination.'

The Declaration was adopted by an overwhelming majority of the General Assembly, with 143 countries voting in support, 4 *voting against, Australia, Canada, New Zealand and the United States.* (UN Permanent Forum on Indigenous Issues)

The one good outcome of this recent move by Canada is that the world stage now knows what we have always known. As Secretary General Ban Ki-moon stated: 'This marks a historic moment when UN Member States and Indigenous peoples reconciled with their painful histories and resolved to move forward together on the path of human rights, justice, and development for all' (UN Permanent Forum on Indigenous Issues). The painful histories he speaks of cannot reconcile when the country of Canada does not even acknowledge the level of human suffering they still inflict on the Lubicon and Haudenosaunee people, and yes, Mr Ole Simel, we do go through hell. It's a hell outlined in this book and it is a hell when the citizens of Canada refuse to acknowledge it even exists. I refer to the impact of our long and painful journey with our colonizers as soul wounds.

Soul Wounds

Throughout my time at Little Buffalo, I could never quite articulate the 'state' the Lubicon people were in, except that it seemed as if the people were attendees at an unending funeral, grieving. Through an Elder named Birgil Kills Straight, I learned of Lakota scholar Maria Brave Heart and her community work on historical trauma, which she borrowed from Jewish Holocaust survivor literature. According to Brave Heart, historical trauma involves 'cumulative trauma – collective and compounding emotional and psychic wounding' (in Niederland 1989), both over the life span and across generations. It involves a constellation of features identified in the literature on post-traumatic stress disorder and psychic trauma (Kystal 1984; van der Kolk 1987). It is associated with reactions to massive generational group trauma. It is unresolved grief over generations of devastating losses and leads to profound, unsettled bereavement (Brave Heart and DeBruyn 1998, 228). She also contends that it is compounded by the dominant society's refusal to acknowledge the genocide that took place and that continues to take place. What would history look like if the Germans had won? Would it look like Canadian history? While the Lubicon and many other nations continue to battle the state and corporations – they must bury the dead, they must carry on. Their strength, *our* strength, comes from our spirituality, our ceremonies, and our land. This book is testimony to that strength, testimony to Indigenous Knowledge and its power. I now know why Chief Bernard did not allow this book to be published for almost á decade: he was concerned with my welfare, that I would be targeted for writing this book. If I told you I have no fear, no anxiety about writing this, I would be lying. I was too young and naive a decade ago to be afraid; since then, since Caledonia, I realize that my status as a Mohawk woman in this country already quadruples my chances of experiencing racialized violence. As a professor, it soars. Don't think for a minute that I have not already been attacked, literally, but that's another book. But fear is what immobilizes us, stay quiet and you won't get hurt. Courage is what many of these past and present Elders provide me with: 'It is the Creator's work' (Henry Joe).

The inspiration for finishing this book came in 2003. The Lubicon children my two eldest daughters played with back in 1992 had all grown up. More than a decade had passed since I considered this research complete. When I returned to Little Buffalo in 2003, those children had children of their own. They shook my hand and asked, 'Where is your book? Did you ever finish it?' I was not sure how to respond except to tell them it was still in progress. In disbelief, they encouraged me to send them the book when it was done. I needed to finish this book for them.

Bernard and Louise's youngest daughter, Melissa, as quiet as could be, one day allowed me to interview her. She shared with me a dream about horses. She said she found them all bloody and dead. But government officials were there bearing gifts. She told me she didn't want their gifts, she only wanted her horses and the land. But more than that, she wanted her community's families to be together and happy. In her young life, she has witnessed tensions, social ills, and family breakdowns. I understood her dream and thought it quite profound. Can any adult step back and simply cherish the simple things in life that are full of spirit?

Back in 1992, Bernard's eldest son, Erwin, and Dwight and Rosanne's sons Jordie and Timothy shared with me their ideas about leadership. They thought there should be three chiefs: a hunting chief; an 'outsider' chief, who would travel; and a stay-at-home chief, who would take care of the people. They had it dead on as far as the Haudenosaunee were concerned. They dreamed of a day when they could have their land and live in peace. One young man, who is no longer with us, had drawn a picture, which his mother showed me. He had drawn a cabin, a sweat lodge and an outhouse, with moose tracks leading into the woods. He had said, 'This is my dream. To have a home, hunt, and do ceremonies, that is all.'

Then there is Jennifer, with whom I remained closest. She is a bright and intelligent Lubicon woman living in harsh circumstances. First she turned twenty, now thirty, and all is still the same – nothing to do. There are days that never end – no money, no jobs, nothing. She was thrilled to land a job at the nurse's trailer driving people to medical appointments. This young mother of four is struggling to keep her sanity as the world around her stands still, caught between what was and what is. All I can do is listen to her, and offer her love and support. It is all quite maddening. She has finished some post-secondary schooling but wonders whether her people will ever have a real health centre and real jobs.

Too many of the children I came to know and love have died. They are the casualties of Canada's relentless assault on the Lubicon Cree. For reasons of ethics, I promised the mothers and fathers of these children that I would not write about their deaths. It would have been too painful for them. The level of grief in the community is at times unbearable – everyone has an open wound. Every new death reminds everyone of the last one, and they all still hurt. There have been many deaths, of young and old, about which I cannot speak. There have been dozens of miscarriages. The women still grieve for their unborn children. They told me they did not want me to talk about how many, they still felt too badly about it. I cannot mention all the Elders who have passed on because their wives and children are still grieving. During my last visit to the community in 2004, I promised I would not write about those beautiful young children who have needlessly passed on, children I deeply cared about. Children I thought were going to become great leaders have been taken from all of us. But I can speak of those who are survivors. For all of you out there with children and families, think of them once in a while and think about Jennifer and what the government needlessly stole from her. To do nothing is to be part of the ongoing assault on this small, struggling Cree community. Finally, for those on the front lines here in my community of Six Nations, your ancestors made these relationships for a reason. Remember, in unity there is strength.

I'll save the last words for the true soul of the Haudenosaunee – our Clanmothers. In July 2007 eight Clanmothers of Six Nations wrote a collective statement for the Haudenosaunee Environmental Forum, titled the 'Haudenosaunee Clanmothers Statement on Land and Environmental Issues' (14 July 2007):

> We give thanks for all of creation with Ga no hon nyo (Thanksgiving Address). We would also like to give thanks and acknowledge the Peacemaker and Ji go sa se the mother of all nations for creating our duties as daughters, sisters, mothers, aunties, grandmothers, and Clanmothers.
>
> Clanmothers have many responsibilities, some of which involve looking after the well-being of our clans and nations. We also have shared responsibilities with the Chiefs and people as caretakers of e ti nwa she ni yo wen ja: deh (everyone's mother, the earth) to respect all of Creation. Respecting the environment is demonstrated when our ceremonies are conducted and within our minds everyday when we give thanks personally to all of life. Our O gwe hon we neha (Our Way of Life) involves the Ga yen neh sra go wa (the Great Law of Peace), our spiritual beliefs/ceremonies, and our moral or ethical codes. All this has survived and continues to thrive despite the intention to assimilate the Haudenosaunee (People of the Longhouse). We also acknowledge our ancestors' strength, as this represents their love and care for us by making the Treaties and land leases thinking of us and our future. They continued the ceremonies and passed on knowledge, wisdom and truth despite the hardships that they endured.
>
> The current environmental adversity e ti nwa she ni yo wen ja: deh is experiencing, has been foretold by our ancestors through prophecy. I'm sure we can recall moments when our ancestors and elders talked about messages from Sohn gwai ya di soh (you who made everything, the Creator). Telling us 'there will come a day when ...,' these statements followed with revelations of changes to environmental aspects, the water, the animals, the plants, and the people. One thing we must not lose sight of is that

we have a choice to do something, to change the direction we are going in. What we encourage is for the people to choose to do their part to help change things for the better. When we uphold our original instructions to respect all of creation and uphold the jurisdiction of the Ga yen neh sra go wa; we are using a good mind to acquire PEACE, when we are being compassionate and helping one another we demonstrate our POWER, when we are honest in our thoughts, words, and actions we have RIGHTEOUS-NESS in our mind, body, and spirit. When we do our best to uphold Ga yen neh sra go wa we demonstrate RESPECT for Sohn gwai ya di soh, our ancestors, ourselves, and are able to share that respect with others and all of Creation.

Continuance of life depends on this sustenance and it is the duty of everyone to nurture and protect the land. As women we have a special relationship to e tin wa se ni yo wen ja: deh because we also give life and nourish the children and the generations that come from us. We are responsible to teach and demonstrate that we are stewards of the natural world. This role must now encompass a much greater struggle that indigenous people all around the world are facing in light of the industrialization and destruction of e tin wa she ni yo wen ja: deh.

We witness an encroachment not only on our lands, but also on our minds and bodies. This is a time when our hearts must grow stronger even though our soil is covered with concrete, our water polluted, and our bodies weakened by disease. Our responsibility is to the coming faces and to the people who are living. As Haudenosaunee people, the Ga yen ne sra go wa holds the power to rectify the abuse and mismanagement of our people, and our traditional lands. As we seek harmony and peace within ourselves, our clans and our nations, we seek harmony and peace within the natural world, which provides us with all that is needed to maintain our communities and further our livelihoods. The Ga ya ne sra go wa granted to us by the Sohn gwai ya di soh harmonized our political system, our spirituality and our e tin wa she ni yo wen ja: deh by creating a society that functioned with the exclusion of greed and dominance.

Due to the genocidal practices and interference of Ha dih nyoh (White people) European society our connection to the natural world has suffered many forms of oppression:
• Cultural Imperialism: the outlawing/restriction and continued devaluing of our spiritual ways, ceremonies, culture, and languages
• Marginalization: forcing our people to live on reservations, the racial discrimination our people continue to experience, exclusion of the truth about Haudenosaunee contributions to the development of Canada

- Violence: the residential school system which raped, beat, murdered, and destroyed our traditional family relationships and the effective way we passed our O gwe hon we ne ha (Our Way of Life), physical and racial violence, sexual assault, harassment, intimidation, and ridicule
- Exploitation: with the dispossession of our lands, the theft of our trust monies, forcing the Indian Act (assimilation policies) on all O gwe hon we people
- Powerlessness: the governments attempt to disband the Haudenosaunee Confederacy in 1924 and the Canadian government's continued disregard of treaty, land, and human rights for all O gwe hon weh people

For many of our people, money is now our connection to sustenance. Our hands and feet don't touch the earth as Sohn gwai ya di soh intended. We no longer drink water from our streams and rivers. Our children are not safe playing outside because of harmful chemicals being sprayed in the air. Foreign entities are being introduced to our ecosystems creating mass devastation amongst our trees and medicines. Our struggle is no longer smallpox, but rather diabetes, cancer, suicide, drugs, alcohol, and violence. More of the Ha dih nyoh (White people) dishonesty, is that our existence is considered a financial burden and drain on the government's purse strings. We are the most expendable people on this land according to Canadian laws and legislation.

With the knowledge and awareness of the effects of global warming, the community took a stand once again just as our ancestors have in the past, to reclaim the green spaces here on the Haldimand Tract. Our intent was not to confine or restrict other people from where they have put their homes or to gain money and material wealth. Our true intention is to bring justice related to our land, tell the true history regarding the manipulation and theft of our inherent rights provided by Sohn gwai ya di soh.

We have experienced a reawakening, our people are growing conscious of their need for spirituality, gaining motivation to learn the ceremonies, traditional languages, and taking a stand to defend and protect one of our most sacred resources, the land. There is no room for hatred or judgment, we must move beyond the anger and look for solutions. Destruction has been put upon us and we choose not to suffer, but rather to live. We must clean the soil, teach our children to survive off the land and grow our traditional foods once again. We must honor and protect all of life, we must speak for our relatives that can't speak, the medicines, the animals, the air, the earth, and the waters. All the generations, the elders, the children, the youth, and the adults must unite as one to help the earth, which in turn helps us and our generations to come. Harmony will come from realizing that we all need each other to grow and that we must help our weakest to stand up again and this includes our relatives in the natural world. The strength that nature shows us when grass grows through concrete, surviving and proving the strength of spirit that comes form Sohn gwai ya di soh, that is within us and connects us to all of creation. The knowledge of our ancestors is being revitalized and we must use it to welcome cycles of change and the coming faces with awareness, peace and pride.

Danetoh (Tekawaennake, 2007)

Kathy Smoke, Cayuga, Bear Clan
Louise McDonald, Mohawk, Bear Clan
Bernice Johnson, Onondaga, Wolf Clan
Mina Key, Cayuga, Snipe Clan
Mary Sandy, Onieda, Bear Clan
Eileen Jacobs, Onondaga, Turtle Clan
Frances Froman, Cayuga, Wolf Clan
Lucille Jamieson, Onondaga, Wolf Clan

References

Published Sources

Akwesasne Notes, ed. 2005. *Basic Call to Consciousness*. Summertown, TN: Native Voices.

Alfred, Taiaiake. 1999. *Peace Power and Righteousness: An Indigenous Manifesto*. Don Mills, ON: Oxford University Press.

Amnesty International. 2004. *Stolen Sisters: Discrimination and Violence against Indigenous Women in Canada*.

Anderson, Kim. 2000. *A Recognition of Being: Reconstructing Native Womanhood*. Toronto: Second Story Press.

Asad, Talal. 1986. 'The Concept of Cultural Translation in British Anthropology.' In *Writing Culture: The Poetics and Politics of Ethnography*, ed. James Clifford and George E. Marcus, 141–64. Berkeley: University of California Press.

Asch, Michael. 1986. 'The Land Claims of the Lubicon Lake People: A Report to the Canadian Ethnology Society.' In *The Bulletin*, ed. Noel Dyck. Burnaby.

Barreiro, Jose, ed. 1992. *Indian Roots of American Democracy*. Ithaca, NY: Akwe:kon Press.

Battiste, Marie, and James Youngblood Henderson. 2000. *Protecting Indigenous Knowledge and Heritage: A Global Challenge*. Saskatoon: Purich Publishing.

Berger, Thomas R. 1977. *Northern Frontier, Northern Homeland: The Report of the Mackenzie Valley Pipeline Inquiry*. Ottawa: Minister of Supply and Services Canada.

– 1991. *A Long and Terrible Shadow: White Values, Native Rights in the Americas, 1492–1992*. Toronto: Douglas and McIntyre.

Berkhofer, Robert. 1979. *The White Man's Indian: Images of the American Indian from Columbus to the Present*. New York: Vintage Books.

Brave Heart, M.Y., and L.M. DeBruyn. 1998. 'The American Indian Holocaust: Healing Historical Unresolved Grief.' *American Indian and Alaska Native Mental Health Research: Journal of the National Center* 8(2): 56–78.

Brody, Hugh. 1981. *Maps and Dreams: A Journey into the Lives and Lands of the Beaver Indians of Northwest Canada*. Toronto: Penguin Books.

Brown, E. Joseph. 1989. *Black Elk: The Sacred Pipe*. Norman: University of Oklahoma Press.

Burke, Kenneth. 1969. *A Grammar of Motives*. Berkeley and Los Angeles: University of California Press.

Cajete, Gregory. 1994. *Look to the Mountain: An Ecology of Indegenous Education*. Durango: Kivaki Press.

– 1999. *Native Science: Natural Laws of Interdependence*. Sante Fe: Clear Light Publishing.

Carter, Sarah. 1990. *Lost Harvests: Prairie Indian Reserve Farmers and Government Policy*. Montreal and Kingston: McGill-Queen's University Press.

– 1996. 'First Nations Women of Prairie Canada in the Early Reserve Years, the 1870s to the 1920s: A Preliminary Inquiry.' In *Women of the First Nations: Power, Wisdom, Strength*, ed. Christine Miller and Patricia Chuckryk with Maria Smallface Marule, Brenda Manyfingers, and Cheryl Deering, 51–76. Winnipeg: University of Manitoba Press.

Castellano, Marlene Brant. 2000. 'Updating Aboriginal Traditions of Knowledge.' In *Indigenous Knowledges in Global Contexts: Multiple Readings of Our World*, ed. G. Dei, B. Hall, and D. Rosenberg, 21–36. Toronto: University of Toronto Press.

Chomsky, Noam. 2003. *Hegemony or Survival: America's Quest for Global Dominance*. New York: Henry Holt.

Churchill, Ward. 1992. *Struggle for the Land: Indigenous Resistance to Genocide, Ecocide, and Expropriation in Contemporary North America*. Toronto: Between the Lines.

– 1997. *A Little Matter of Genocide: Holocaust and Denial in the Americas 1492 to the Present*. San Francisco: City Lights Books.

Clifford, James. 1983. 'On Ethnographic Authority.' *Representations* 1(2): 132–43.

Clifford, James, and George E. Marcus, eds. 1986. *Writing Culture: The Poetics and Politics of Ethnography*. Berkeley and Los Angeles: University of California Press.

Coon Come, Matthew, 30 May 1992 Presentation to the Drum Beat Conference, McMaster University, Hamilton.

– 1995. *Sovereign Injustice: Forcible Inclusion of the James Bay Cree Territory into a Sovereign Quebec*. Quebec: Grand Council of the Crees.

Cummins, John, and Bryan Steckler. 2001. *Full Circle: Canada's First Nations.* Scarborough: Prentice Hall.

Daes, Erica-Irene. 1994. *Protection of Heritage of Indigenous People* (Daes Report). New York: UN.

Davis, Wade. 2000. *Light at the Edge of the World: A Journey through the Realm of Vanishing Cultures.* Vancouver: Douglas and McIntyre.

Dei, George, Budd Hall, and Dorothy Rosenberg, eds. 2000. *Indigenous Knowledge in Global Contexts: Multiple Readings of Our World.* Toronto: University of Toronto Press.

Deloria, Vine. 1994. *God Is Red: A Native View of Religion.* Golden: Fulcrum Publishing.

– 1997. *Red Earth White Lies: Native Americans and the Myth of Scientific Fact.* Golden: Fulcrum Publishing.

Deloria, Vine, and James Treat. 1999. *For This Land: Writings on Religion in America.* New York: Routledge.

Dickason, Olive Patricia. 1992. *Canada's First Nations: A History of Founding Peoples from Earliest Times.* Toronto: McClelland and Stewart.

Dobyns, H.F. 1983. *Their Number Became Thinned: Native American Population Dynamics in Eastern North America.* Knoxville: University of Tennessee Press.

Drysdale, Vera. L., and Joseph E. Brown. 1953. *The Gift of the Sacred Pipe: Based on Black Elk's Account of the Seven Rites of the Oglala Souix.* Norman: University of Oklahoma Press.

Dumont, James. 1976. 'Journey to Daylight Land.' Unpublished paper, University of Sudbury.

Duran, E., and B. Duran. 1995. *Native American Postcolonial Psychology.* New York: SUNY Press.

Durkheim, Émile. 1933. *The Division of Labor in Society.* New York: Free Press.

Fournier, Suzanne, and Ernie Crey. 1997. *Stolen from Our Embrace: The Abduction of First Nations Children and the Restoration of Aboriginal Communities.* Vancouver: Douglas and McIntyre.

Frideres, James S., and Rene R. Gadacz. 2005. *Aboriginal People in Canada: Contemporary Conflicts.* Toronto: Prentice Hall.

Fulton, David. 1986. 'Lubicon Lake Indian Band – Inquiry.' Unpublished discussion paper Vancouver, February.

Goddard, John. 1985. 'Last Stand of the Lubicon Cree.' *Equinox* (May–June), 67–77.

– 1991. *Last Stand of the Lubicon Cree.* Vancouver: Douglas and McIntyre.

Grace, S.L. 2002. 'Aboriginal Women.' In *Ontario Women's Health Status Report.* Toronto: OWHC.

Green, Rayna, and Howard Bass. 1998. 'Heartbeat II.' Audiocassette. 79 minutes. Washington: Smithsonian Folkways.

Gunn Allen, Paula. 1986. *The Sacred Hoop: Recovering the Feminine in American Indian Traditions*. Boston: Beacon Press.

Hill, Dawn. 1992. *As Snow before the Summer Sun: An Exhibit on Our Relationship to the Natural Environment*. Brantford, ON: Woodland Cultural Centre.

Jaimes, M. Annette, ed. 1992. *The State of Native America: Genocide, Colonization, and Resistance*. Boston: South End Press.

Larocque, Sylvain. 2006. 'Canada Stalling UN Declaration on Indigenous Rights: Amnesty International.' Canadian Press, 20 June 2006.

Lennerson, Fred. 1988. 'The Lubicon Lake Nation Cree.' Unpublished paper, Edmonton.

Lubicon Settlement Commission of Review. 1993. *The Lubicon Settlement Commission of Review: Final Report*. Edmonton.

Lux, Maureen, K. 2001. *Medicine That Walks: Disease, Medicine, and Canadian Plains Native People*. Toronto: University of Toronto Press.

Lyons, Oren, and John Mohawk, eds. 1992. *Exiled in the Land of the Free: Democracy, Indian Nations, and the U.S. Constitution*. Sante Fe: Clear Light.

Mandelbaum, David G. 1979. *The Plains Cree: An Ethnographic, Historical, and Comparative Study.* Regina: Canadian Plains Research Center.

Martin-Hill, Dawn. 1992. Statement from the Lubicon Lake Nation Women's Circle. December.

– 1995. 'Lubicon Lake Nation Spirit of Resistance.' PhD dissertation, McMaster University.

McGillivray, A., and B. Comaskey. 1999. *Black Eyes All of the Time: Intimate Violence, Aboriginal Women, and the Justice System*. Toronto: University of Toronto Press.

Meili, Dianne. 1991. *Those Who Know: Profiles of Alberta's Native Elders*. Edmonton: NeWest Press.

Miller, C. and P. Chuckryk. 1996. *Women of the First Nations: Power, Wisdom, and Strength*. Winnipeg: University of Manitoba Press.

Monture-Angus, P. 1995. *Thunder in My Soul: A Mohawk Women Speaks*. Halifax: Fernwood Publishing.

– 1999. *Journeying Forward: Dreaming First Nations' Independence*. Halifax: Fernwood Publishing.

Morrison, R. Bruce, and R.C. Wilson. 1986. *Native Peoples: The Canadian Experience*. Toronto: McClelland and Stewart.

Norris, M., M. Cooke, D. Beavon, E. Guimond, and S. Clathworth. 2003. 'Registered Indian Mobility and Migration in Canada.' In *Population, Mobility, and Indigenous Peoples in Australasia and North America*, ed. J. Taylor and M. Bell. New York: Routledge.

Perez, Fernando Hernandez. 1998. *Aboriginal Voices* 5.

Persky, Stan. 1998. *Delgamuukw: The Supreme Court of Canada Decision on Aboriginal Title*. Vancouver: Douglas and McIntyre.

Rabinow, Paul. 1986. 'Representations Are Social Facts: Modernity and Post-Modernity in Anthropology.' In *Writing Culture: The Poetics of Ethnography*, ed. James Clifford and George E. Marcus, 234–61. Berkeley and Los Angeles: University of California Press.

Richardson, Boyce. 1989. *Drumbeat: Anger and Renewal in Indian Country*. Toronto: Summerhill Press.

Rosaldo, Renato. 1989. *Culture and Truth: The Remaking of Social Analysis*. Boston: Beacon Press.

Royal Commission on Aboriginal Peoples (RCAP). 1997. *Report of the Royal Commission on Aboriginal People*. Volume 3. *Gathering Strength*. Ottawa: RCAP.

Ryan, Joan. 1990. 'United Nations: International Covenant on Civil and Political Rights.' Human Rights Committee, 38th Session. CCPR/C/38/D/167/ 1984. 28 March.

Said, Edward. 1989. 'Representing the Colonized: Anthropology's Interlocutors.' *Critical Inquiry* 15: 205–25.

St Pierre, Mark, and Tilda Long Soldier: 1995. *Walking in the Sacred Manner: Healers, Dreamers, and Pipe Carriers*. New York: Touchstone.

Sioui, George. 1992. *For an Amerindian Autohistory*. Montreal and Kingston: McGill-Queen's University Press.

Smith, James. 1987. 'The Western Woods Cree: Anthropological Myth and Historical Reality.' *American Ethnologist* 14(3): 434–48.

– 1988. 'Canada: The Lubicon Lake Cree.' *Cultural Survival Quarterly* 11(3): 61–2.

Smith, Linda Tuhiwai. 1999. *Decolonizing Methodologies: Research and Indigenous Peoples*. London: Zed Books.

Titley, E. Brian. 1986. *A Narrow Vision: Duncan Campbell Scott and the Administration of Indian Affairs in Canada*. Vancouver: UBC Press.

Trinh, Minh Ha. 1989. *Woman, Native, Other: Writing Postcoloniality and Feminism*. Bloomington: Indiana University Press.

Van der Kolk, B.A. 1987. *Psychological Trauma*. Arlington: American Psychiatric Publishing.

Van Kirk, Sylvia. 1980. *Many Tender Ties: Women in Fur-Trade Society, 1670–1870*. Norman: University of Oklahoma Press.

Vecsey, C. 1996. *On the Padres' Trail: American Indian Catholics*. Notre Dame: University of Notre Dame Press.

Venne, Sharon. 1998. *Our Elders Understand Our Rights: Evolving International Law Regarding Indigenous Rights*. Penticton, BC: Theytus Press.

Waldram, James B., Ann Herring, and T. Kue Young. 1997. *Aboriginal Health in*

Canada: Historical, Cultural, and Epidemiological Perspectives. Toronto: University of Toronto Press.

Weatherford, Jack. 1988. *Indian Givers: How the Indians of the Americas Transformed the World.* New York: Crown Publishing.

Wearne, P. 1996. *Return of the Indian: Conquest and Revival in the Americas.* London: Continuum.

Wesley-Esquimaux, Cynthia, and Magdalena Smolewsky. 2004. *Historic Trauma and Aboriginal Healing.* Ottawa: Aboriginal Healing Foundation.

Wright, Ronald. 1992. *Stolen Continents: The New World through Indian Eyes since 1492.* Toronto: Viking.

York, Geoffrey, and Loreen Pindera. 1992. *People of the Pines: The Warriors and the Legacy of Oka.* Toronto: McArthur and Co.

Interviews and Personal Communication

****, Alice. October 1992.

Auger, Maggie. November 1992.

Auger, Simon. August 1991.

Henry Joe, 1992.

Gladue, Dwight. January 1991.

Gladue, Dwight. July 1991.

Gladue, Dwight. April 1993.

Henry Joe. 1989, 1991, August 1992.

John 'C.' July 1991, June 1992.

Laboucon, Albert. December 1989.

Laboucon, Edward. October 1989.

Latendre, John. 1991, 1992.

Ominayak, Bernard. 1989, 1991, June 1992, 2000.

Ominayak, Jennifer. November 1992.

Ominayak, Louisa. December 1992.

Ominayak, Louise. December 1989, June 1991, July 1992.

Sowan, Rosanne. August 1991.

Whitehead, Lillian. June 1992.

Whitehead, Walter. October 1989, April 1990, January 1991, August 1992.

Index